CONCILIUM

concilium 1995/6

RELIGION AND NATIONALISM

Edited by

John Coleman and
Miklós Tomka

SCM Press · London
Orbis Books · Maryknoll

Published by SCM Press Ltd, 9–17 St Albans Place, London N1
and by Orbis Books, Maryknoll, NY 10545

ISBN: 0 334 030358 (UK)
ISBN: 0 88344 887 4 (USA)

Typeset at The Spartan Press Ltd, Lymington, Hants
Printed by Mackays of Chatham, Kent

Concilium Published February, April, June, August, October, December.

Contents

Editorial   The Challenge of Nationalism to the Churches
JOHN COLEMAN and MIKLÓS TOMKA   vii

I · Nationalism in History and Church History   3

Confession and Political Identity in Europe at the Beginning of
Modern Times (Fifteenth to Eighteenth Centuries)   3
  HEINZ SCHILLING
Universal Christian Faith and Nationalism   14
  VICTOR CONZEMIUS
Secularization and Nationalism   22
  MIKLÓS TOMKA

II · Patriotism, Nationalism and the Duties of Citizens   33
Patriotism and Nationalism   33
  HEINRICH SCHNEIDER
A Nation of Citizens   48
  JOHN COLEMAN

III · The Role of Religion in National Conflicts   59
Religion and Churches in the Post-Yugoslav War   59
  SRDJAN VRCAN
Religion, Nationalism and the Break-Up of Canada   68
  DAVID SELJAK
De profundis . . . The Religions as the Support of Minorities   77
  LÁSZLÓ ASZÓDI and FRATER GEORGIUS

IV · Religion and Nationalism World-Wide   87
What Kind of Nationalism? Ethical Distinctions   87
  GREGORY BAUM

Secularism, Hindu Nationalism and the Fear of People   96
  ASHIS NANDY
Islam and Nationalism   103
  ZIAUDDIN SARDAR

Contributors   111

Editorial: The Challenge of Nationalism to the Churches

Is nationalism an achievement of Christian culture (a questionable one)? Is it nourished by that way of thinking which accords earthly things, and thus society and politics, a high degree of independence? Is the national then so powerful that it can harness religion and the churches to its own carriage? And conversely, do the Christian churches nurture a form of community orientated on tradition which feels most at home and secure in a national homogenous, perhaps a nationalistic, culture? But is not nationalism one of those group egotisms which then deny the universalism of Christianity, and which in principle conflict with the gospel? Is it not the cause and source of countless inhumanities? Or do discrimination and oppression have other roots, and is nationalism the attempt to gain emancipation from them and struggle for one's own freedom and identity? It is doubtful whether there are single timeless answers to these questions independent of any situation. So in what follows, alongside attempts at interpretation on a theoretical level, there are historical analyses and studies of countries, and the context of Islam and Hinduism and the views of minorities are all illuminated.

The nation in the modern sense and the national are relatively recent social facts. However, they have a prehistory as principles of political order. The word 'nation' is by no means new, but in antiquity and even in the Middle Ages it had a different significance. This development is traced in the articles by Conzemius, Schilling and Tomka. In Schilling's view nationalism is closely connected with confessionalization, already before the Reformation (in Spain), and then on a European scale as a result of the Reformation. In that case nationalism would be the fruit of a development in which the translation of Christian universalism into politics failed. This chronological contextualizing is also shared by others and at most modified to the degree that Conzemius and Schneider see the period of the schisms over faith more as a preliminary phase to nationalism, putting the rise of nationalism proper at the time of the Enlightenment (Conzemius) or the

French Revolution (Schneider). It is a wider question (thus in Tomka) whether the nationalism of confessionalizing is to be identified with the nationalism of the secularized era. Perhaps from the beginning nationalism has been a 'construct to provide a substitute for religion' (Schneider). But perhaps it has become a pseudo-religion only in the modern, post-Christian period as a result of the function of religion in integrating society and supporting culture.

Painful experiences in the present may motivate us to regard any kind of nationalism, perhaps even nationalistic feelings, critically and with mistrust. If the term nationalism conveys a conviction of national superiority, a sweeping repudiation is understandable (thus in Vrcan). If nationalism is simply responsibility for one's own society, it has a positive emphasis (in Coleman). However, in this second case there is automatically a distinction between a 'normal' nationalism and an exaggerated nationalism, or a good nationalism and a bad nationalism. That also raises the question of how, when and why the one form turns into the other. Schneider offers a fundamental article on the history of the term, the functions of nationalism and the connections between nationalism and the nation state. He explains the distinction between nation states and national cultures which is fundamental to the formation of European states and also to some present-day conficts. Here the illegitimacy of claims to absoluteness both by the state (or the nation state) or the ethnic, culturally defined group (national culture) becomes evident. Constitutional patriotism is indicated as a solution. This notion is pursued further by Coleman. He regards the nation state and also nationalism as valuable and indispensable structures which help towards an emotional-affective and a symbolic integration. However, nationalism as a necessary structural principle of modern societies must be combined with democracy and realized in the networks of civil society if it is to be able to become the motive force for civic virtues. Democracy cannot function without a perception of duties towards the nation. And where this democracy guarantees the same rights to all, including minorities, the excesses of nationalism will be prevented.

The role of religion and the churches in national conflicts is the concern of three studies. Against the background of the atrocities in former Yugoslavia Vrcan castigates the churches for their involvement in nationalisms. He asks a fundamental question. Does religion distort or illuminate cosmic and ontological orders? Does this position not necessarily lead to an absolutizing of social differences and tend towards a Manichaean black-and-white view of things? A second programmatic question which he asks is whether the post-Communist churches – by nature? – tend to favour the framework of the nation states and national cultural and social structures to secure their own futures. In the middle of the war in Bosnia and Croatia it is not surprising that Vrcan emphasizes the negative sides of nationalism. From Quebec in Canada Seljak offers another view. He is concerned with the nurturing of cultural identity, the right to national self-determination and to resistance against oppression. Nationalism then becomes the vehicle of 'conscientization', political participation and education to social responsibility. He assigns a fundamentally positive role to the Catholic Church both in its commitment to the right of self-determination and also its concern for respect for the demands of human dignity, readiness for reconciliation and the subordination of nationalism to the common good and solidarity with the needy. Aszódi and Frater report a third instance. The national minorities (e.g. in Roumania) are made separate groups as a result of the discrimination against them, and they can preserve their culture only by cultivating their distinctive characteristics. Here, therefore, is a nationalism imposed by the situation which in view of the people and culture also includes religion. Does the church here have any other alternative than to take its stand alongside the oppressed? But even if this option is indisputable, must not the church systematically and in an institutional form stand up for reconciliation? Like Seljak and Vrcan, Aszódi and Frater also find fault with the efforts of the church in this connection.

Baum presents Buber's, Gandhi's and Tillich's views on nationalism. These three outstanding figures lay the conservative religious foundation for the ethical justification of nationalism. They call for reflection and for a return to cultural roots, and the conscious acceptance of a common (national) past and future. But they no less require the cultivation of spiritual values and the recognition of the over-riding importance of social justice. The nations are to serve human well-being. Contrary to Gandhi, for Nandy nationalism is fundamentally in conflict with Hinduism. He sees nationalism as a corrupt product of modernization and secularization. In his view nationalism is an ideology of the urban middle classes which holds out no prospects for the future. Sardar argues in a somewhat similar way in the Islamic context. For him, nationalism is part of the Western project of modernization, but also a response to colonization and an attempt to preserve identity. He derives nationalism and Islamic fundamentalism from the same roots, but regards both as anti-Islamic and as dead ends. This repudiation in principle is not affected by forecasts that there will also presumably be waves of nationalism in coming years in areas which have become free or which are still not free, in Central Asia and in China.

Nationalism is a social, political matter. Is it a concern of the churches? Even churches which want to lead a ghetto existence cannot avoid the effects of national and nationalistic tensions. If the church proclaims the good news in and for this world, if it takes the independent structures of this world seriously, it must grapple with the causes and consequences of nationalism. But in particular if the church is to be a sacrament of unity, it must also accept the practical consequences, and oppose all forms of disunity. These include any nationalism which consists only in the perpetuation of specific charismas and also leads to the humiliation of other individuals and groups. Nationalism is a challenge to the church.

John Coleman
Miklós Tomka

I · Nationalism in History and Church History

Confession and Political Identity in Europe at the Beginning of Modern Times (Fifteenth to Eighteenth Centuries)[1]

Heinz Schilling

I The sociological and confessional foundations of modern Europe

Nowadays an investigation into the connection between religious and political identity hardly requires explicit legitimation. In the present day, what the war of Christian Serbs or Croats against Muslim Bosnians in former Yugoslavia has in common with comparable conflicts in the former Soviet Union, especially between Armenians and Azerbaijanis, and the explosive interlocking of religious, ethnic and social forces on the Indian continent, to mention only the most striking instances, is all too clear. We might also think of the Ukraine, where the tense rivalry between Russian Orthodoxy, the autocephalous Ukrainian Orthodox Church and the Ukrainian Catholic Church, while not affecting – as far as I can see – the formation of internal national identity – does have a key influence on the question of orientation in foreign politics; its resolution in one direction or another will have a vital long-term influence on the identity of the country and the recently freed Ukrainian nation, as either linked primarily eastwards with Orthodox Russia or orientated on the West via the Roman Catholic Poles.

Quite apart from current topical issues, already in the middle of the 1970s historians were again turning to questions related to the sociology of religion: at a time when even non-Marxist historiography was predominantly interested in social and economic forces, and religious and cultural factors generally had largely faded into background, it was important to establish the historical relevance of religion and the church to the rise of modern European societies. Distinctions needed to be made in two directions, theoretically and methodologically, on the one hand against the sociological reductionism of a history which had no religious and cultural explanatory models, and on the other against an idealism which was no less reductionist, to which any form of sociological interpretation of religious and church phenomena was suspect. Indeed, in some theological faculties at the time one could note an insistence that church history had to investigate only the actions of God within a process defined by salvation history. Two strands of the sociological discussion were helpful in constructing a sociological and confessional historical approach which both avoided reductionism and understood religion as an independent and effective factor in and through history: the debate on modernization going back to Max Weber, and the systems-theoretical approach.

In the systems-theoretical perspective the period of the Reformation, and to some degree also the Middle Ages, can be understood as a social system in which, in contrast to the modern, secularized world of the nineteenth and twentieth centuries, religion and church did not work as sub-systems among other sub-systems but as central and supportive structural axes of society, without which political and social life were not yet fully functional. Jurists of the seventeenth century reduced this to the maxim *religio vinculum societatis* – religion is the bond which unites society, without which ordered life in state and society is impossible. This sociological structural characteristic of early Europe is thus based on the concept of the politics peculiar to that time: in contrast to that of today, it included religion and the church, and did not seek to distance them as external factors alien to politics, as has been customary since the Enlightenment. It follows from this that accurate insights into the rise of modernity cannot be achieved without taking into account confessions as one of the 'basic categories' of historical research.

The reception of the Max Weber debate, not only its thesis of Calvinism but also and above all its thesis of rationality, brought explicit perspectives of historical development into play. It showed the religious and church structures of the beginnings of modernity (fifteenth to seventeenth century), and more markedly those of the confessional age, as the Reformation in the narrower sense, no longer as anachronistic hindrances to social change but, on the contrary, as one of its motive forces. The process of confessionalization here is no longer viewed as a lapse into pre-modern, pre-secular conditions which had 'intrinsically' already become overcome by humanism and the Renaissance. Rather, confessionalization was decidedly understood as modernization, not only – as had along been customary in the wake of Max Weber's thesis about Calvinism – Reformed Protestantism and Protestant dissent, but also Lutheranism and renewed Catholicism. The Reformed movement, Lutheranism and Catholic confessionalizing, were understood in strict systematically conceptual parallelism as processes which were the same or at least similar functionally, i.e. in their macro-historically political and social functions and effects.

'Confessionalizing' means a fundamental sociological process of change which includes changes in the church and religion and in culture and mentality, as well as in state politics and society. Thus it is not only concerned with the rise of the modern confessional churches as institutions or of the confessions as a religious cultural system which clearly differ from one another in doctrine, spirituality, rites and everyday culture. Rather, it is also concerned with a process of change and formation governed by religion and the church, which embraced all spheres of public and private life and left an essential stamp on the profile of modern Europe. Investigation of this confessionalizing embraces an extraordinary wide area – from political, legal and institutional problems, through questions of norms for mentality and conduct (social discipline and church discipline), to the role of the confessional in foreign politics and in the formation of a system of international powers.

II Confessional and political identity in early modern Europe – a birds'-eye view

The specific question of the interplay of confessionalization and the origin or reinforcement of political and especially national identities in early modern Europe, with which we shall be concerned, concerns both mentality and social psychology and law and institutions, that is, the processes of forming both nations and the early modern state. The two could coincide, but they could also go separate ways or even come into conflict. Accordingly, confessional identity could play a role both in the formation of a national consciousness as the basis of a nation-state consciousness and in the formation of political and national identities without forming a state, or in opposition to the formation of a foreign national state. The latter was the case in Ireland, and for a time also in Bohemia, Hungary and Slovenia, during the period of Protestant opposition to the Catholic rule of Hapsburg Austria. Confessional elements also frequently played a part in the formation of minority identities. These were often, but by no means always, in fundamental opposition to a particular state. A minority identity or fundamental opposition was developed, for example by the Catholics in the Netherlands and in England or the Protestants in eighteenth-century France.

The political institutional change in the real-historical formation of the state was matched at the level of collective mentalities by the development of political and cultural identities, which in some European countries assumed the character of national identity at a very early stage. This process, too, which began in the high Middle Ages, was decisively encouraged by the modern confessionalization of the late sixteenth and seventeenth centuries. In a systematic perspective it can be explained in terms of the precarious and revolutionary change from the mediaeval universalist basis for the co-existence of large groups to the modern particularist basis, and the redefinition of self-understanding which went with this. In this transitional phase it was helpful, indeed necessary, for development that the particular understanding of 'we' as relating to individual European states, which was in process of developing, could be based on the universalist discourse of the early modern confessional system, which had a monopoly of the explanation of the world with a transcendental basis.

In post-Reformation Europe four zones of the formation of confessional political identity can be distinguished: the Tridentine Catholic, the Lutheran Protestant, the Reformed Protestant and the mixed or multi-confessional. That there was no formation of national, state identity on the basis of non-confessional religious communities, like the Anabaptists, is significant and confirms my hypothesis that the coupling of the formation of confession and national identity is structurally conditioned. For reasons of space, in what follows I can sketch out only two examples, one from the Catholic and one from the Lutheran zone. However, I should emphasize that the modern historical relationship between confessional and national identity is extraordinary complex and has different strata in each individual instance. It was especially complicated in the fourth zone of mixed or multi-confessional identity, which included above all Germany and Switzerland.[2]

On the Catholic side, the connections are strongest in the case of Spain, where for centuries national awareness and Catholicity, in the confessionalist Tridentine form, was almost the same. That is doubtless connected with the fact that Iberian society experienced its political and cultural hey-day at the same time as confessionalization. The collective recollection of the 'siglo de oro' of Spanish painting and literature and Spain's position of hegemony in Europe and overseas was and is necessarily combined with that of the renewal of Catholicism as a response to the challenge of the Reformation. Spaniards were prominent agents of this renewal in all fields, the spiritual and intellectual as well as the institutional and the political. If the Spaniards regarded the Reformation as *pestis Germaniae*, in their eyes the Counter-Reformation and Catholic renewal were cures for the body of Christianity to the preparation of which the Spanish people had made a decisive contribution – through the religious and organizational genius of its spirtual leaders, above all Ignatius of Loyola; through the ardent faith of the great mystics Teresa of Avila and John of the Cross; through the intellectual acuteness of late scholasticism in universities and learned monasteries (Bartolomé de las Casas, Francisco de Vitoria, Fray Luis de Léon, Luis de Molin, Francisco Suarez); through the political and military resolution of the dynasty and of the church hierarchy and the leading classes generally. All these were elite phenomena which nevertheless deeply influenced the Spanish self-understanding generally. Renewed Catholicism also had great power to form a basis for identity as the result of a popular and everyday culture which was more strongly stamped by confessionalist Catholicism than that of most other European nations; by the mass of brothers and sisters in the Spanish convents of the renewed orders in the other country and throughout the world; and by the sacrifices of men and money which took all Spaniards right across the social strata for generations into the army and the fleet in order to establish the power and glory of the Catholic church along with the renown of Spain in Europe and overseas. Rough and undisciplined though the Spanish soldiers of the confessional era may have been, the battles against the heretics on the European battlefields contributed just as decisively to the formation of national identity as the campaigns overseas, which in addition to the craze for gold and adventurism were also borne up by a missionary ethos: 'Sancta Maria', this battle cry of the Spaniards in 1620 in the battle of the White Mountain in front of Prague, shows how the Spanish soldiers and with them most of their countrymen saw themselves as knights of the Mother of God. Seventy-five years earlier, in the battle of Mühlberg which ended the Schmalkald War, the battle-cry had still simply been 'Hispania and the Empire'. The identification with the Mother of God was a result of Tridentine confessionalization in the wake of which the

Marian piety of the renewed church became the 'ideological nucleus' for the early modern Spanish nation.

This strong and comparatively close identification with the Catholicity of Western Christianity had many roots – political, as above all in the resolute option of the Hapsburgs and the nobility for the battle of faith at home and abroad, and theological and church-historical, as above all in the early, sometimes even pre-Reformation, beginnings of a spiritual and institutional renewal of the Spanish church, which produced visible successes already in the first half of the sixteenth century that were to prove so critical for the Catholic Church everywhere in Europe. However, the most significant presupposition for the close coupling of a nationalistic Spanish and a confessionalistic Catholic self-understanding was probably the late mediaeval experience. In the war against the Arabs in Granada which shaped the militancy and politicization of Christianity far more decisively than early phases of the Reconquista, the religious argument had already openly become a national one. When in 1494 Granada, the last bastion of Islam in Western Europe, fell, the Spanish king and queen, who for the first time united all Spanish countries under one crown, had the honorific title 'Los Reyes Católicos' bestowed on them by Pope Alexander VI. The clash with the strong Jewish minority, which was faced with the choice of converting to Christianity or leaving Spain, also had similar consequences in shaping this mentality.

Thus on the Iberian peninsula at the end of the sixteenth century, religion as the nucleus of collective identity already had a long tradition. The power and explosiveness of this combination had been experienced with opponents who over decades, under the standards of Islam or Judaism, opposed subjection and integration into the rising national society, even if – as was quite rightly suspected – they allowed themselves formally to be converted to Christianity. And Spain had experienced the integrating power of religion in its own ranks, which in reflection on Christianity as the common faith of all Spaniards took on a hitherto unknown cohesion.

This 'ideological' bond was all the more important since the Spanish kingdoms remained institutionally separated throughout the whole of early modernity. Religion and church were the most important over-arching authorities alongside the dynasty. This was of the utmost importance for the political change from late mediaeval to modern forms: the alliance between religion and the formation of the early modern state which elsewhere in Europe took place only in the confessional period was already complete in the Spanish kingdoms under the aegis of late mediaeval

Catholicity. Faced with the task of bringing together the long separated kingdoms and thus bridging deeply-rooted social, institutional and cultural contrasts, the crown had set out on a programme of Christian renewal in order to modernize the part-kingdoms politically and to bring together their inhabitants in one nation under the standard of Catholicity. At the request of the Spaniards, Pope Sixtus IV gave decisive support to the Inquisition established in 1478, one of the first institutions of a Spanish nationalistic kind. Its task was to prevent a feared subversion by 'defeated' *conversos* who had only adopted Christian faith in appearance, but in truth continued to be adherents of Islam or Judaism and thus threatened Christianity from within. The later mediaeval Inquisition, which was recognized by the great majority of the people, had already made the Spaniards familiar with the idea that with pure Christian doctrine at the same time the stability and indeed the existence of state and society were at stake. They had also learned to accept that iron measures were necessary to safeguard this religious and national integrity – executions and expulsions by the thousand.

Religio vinculum societatis – nowhere in Europe was this maxim of the confessional age more familiar than in Spain, where already in the late Middle Ages the bond of Christian religion served as a guarantee of inward unity and outward demarcation from other groups which were felt to be alien, and the otherness of these aliens had been experienced primarily as religious otherness. 'Limpieza de sangre', the ethnic purity of all members of the nation, about which the Spaniards had been concerned since the beginning of the fifteenth century, at the same time always meant purity in Christian doctrine. Thus the late Middle Ages in Spain were dominated not by the widespread search for personal salvation, as we know to be the case in Germany, and which led to the breakthrough of the Reformation, but by a collective will to guarantee the purity of doctrine and ward off any hint of heresy, indeed to make such hints impossible for the future. This early identification of dogmatic purity in the sense of the papal church with national consciousness explains the amazing immunity of the Spaniards as a people to the Reformation, as compared with the rest of Europe. It also explains the identification of national interests with those of modern confessionalist Catholicism which was made at the end of the sixteenth century as a matter of course and which then continued down to the nineteenth and twentieth centuries.

The Scandinavian countries are impressive examples of Lutheran confessional identity. Here, though, we must leave out the Lutheran Germanic territories as special cases, since they were incorporated into the mixed confessional Holy Roman Empire. That applies as much to Denmark as it does to Norway and Sweden. Since in those decades Danes and Swedes were bitter rivals for predominance in the Baltic and in these battles both constantly entered into alliances with non-Lutheran powers – Sweden as a rule with Catholic France and Denmark with the Calvinistic Nether-lands – once again it becomes particularly clear in this North European area that confessional and foreign political fronts did not necessarily have to run in parallel. The discovery of confessional and cultural identity in Lutheranism did not decisively disrupt this either in Sweden or in Denmark – Norway – any more than it did in the case of France on the Catholic side.

In some respects Sweden is the Lutheran counterpart to Spain in the Catholic camp. For here, too, identification with the Reformation caused comparatively little friction and soon had no real alternative; the Lutheran confessionalization became a decisive support both for the formation of the early modern state and for the rise of the European great power. This coupling was of considerable historical significance; perhaps even more important were the consequences for the collective mentality and national awareness of the Swedes, who constantly connected their entry into modern times and the history of internal and eternal success that it sparked off with the Reformation and Lutheran confessionalizing.

The precondition for this development was the traditionally close cultural relations in the area of the Baltic and north-east Germany, which had put the Swedes directly within the sphere of the influence of the Wittenberg Reformation. The link between Lutheranism and national identity was decisively consolidated and ideologized politically somewhat later in the confrontation with the Catholic Wasa line in Poland and in the Thirty Years' War. In the opposition of the Scandinavian kingdom to the efforts at union or, better, annexation, of the converted main line of his dynasty which had attained to the Polish throne, for the younger Swedish Wasa monarchy founded by Count Charles (IX) of Södermanland (1600/4–1611), the father of Gustav Adolf, the Lutheran confession became the decisive argument for his dynastic and political legitimacy. From then on, the Lutheranism of the crown was an ingredient of the Swedish fundamental laws – and thus a direct parallel to the development on the Catholic side in France. For generations, for the ruling classes and their subjects, Reformation and nation were almost inseparable, and thus became the focal point of inner cohesion and concern for independence and self-assertion.

In the Thirty Years' War, which Sweden waged more decisively than the countries as a battle for the Reformation, the still largely mediaeval peasant society underwent a lightning economic and political modernization. At the same time it succeeded in leaping into the very front rank of the European great powers. This experience of success was combined with the myth of Gustav Adolf, the hero of the faith, who in the fighting, understood in eschatological terms, was the Protestant figure of light conquering the powers of darkness and the anti-Christ. This mixture of real historical-political interests and a religious and confessional sense of mission produced that certainty of identity and missionary ethos which gave Sweden inner stability and an expansionist dynamic abroad until the eighteenth century, and also helped it to overcome the deep crisis which the conversion of Queen Christina, the daughter of Gustav Adolf, threatened to bring to state and society in the middle of the seventeenth century.

For large stretches of the nineteenth century Lutheran confessional and Swedish national identity were hardly separable, and institutionally, too, the Swedish state and the Lutheran episcopal church were closely connected. The consequences are evident down to our day – politically and institutionally, and above all in the collective attitude and self-understanding. In a secularized form the Lutheran Reformation ethos still gives Swedish society today the certainty that it is on the right way, coupled with a sense of duty that it must 'convert' the rest of the world to this. It is the secularized Lutheran identity which determines the historically political culture and the moral awareness of the 'nation' today. And even the structure of individual personality seems to be shaped by this – at any rate in the self-interpretation of leading intellectuals. One need only recall the film director Ingmar Bergman, who makes the Lutheran identity responsible for its neuroses.

III Confessional identity as a transitional phenomenon between mediaeval and modern secular identity

In its epoch-making interconnection with the political pressures towards identification and the offers of identity made by the early modern state and the national societies which were forming, the confessional identity of the early modern period in the rising early modern states and their partially already early national peoples, which has been sketched out above more than described in detail, was a transitional type of identification. Confessional identity was the early form of a relatively uniform collective awareness of being 'us' which already was in sharp, 'total' contrast to other awarenesses of being 'us' which had the same structure, in Europe or even in one and the same society. Thus it lies between mediaeval and modern forms of identity. This early modern confessional identity followed chronologically and developmentally the identity models of the high Middle Ages, which were characterized by the problem of a quest for identity and a discovery of identity within the framework of the normative concepts of identity held by the nobility and religion (which was still uniformly Christian), and by the beginnings of reflection on and the relativization of collective identities. The confessional identity of the sixteenth and seventeenth centuries was then followed by the identity problems of the Enlightenment in the eighteenth century and the modern nation states in the nineteenth. The Enlightenment was concerned with the human constitution as a moral subject in tension with traditional structures of society and the development of a distinctive norm of action. The nineteenth century then saw the modern, secular national identity of more recent modernity, in which the confessional and religious elements of the early modern-premodern identity were transcended dialectically. Its radicality and efficiency cannot be understood without the religious background of these earlier confessional identities, which were taken up into it.

Translated by John Bowden

Notes

1. Because of the limited space available, I shall just make a general reference to some of my works which have extensive bibliographies: Heinz Schilling, 'Nationale Identität und kulturelle Identität', in *Studien zur Entwicklung des kollektiven Bewusstseins in der Neuzeit*, ed. Bernhard Giesen, Frankfurt 1991, 192–252; id., 'Luther, Loyola, Calvin und die europäische Neuzeit', *Archiv für Reformationsgeschichte* 85, 1994, 5–31; id., 'Confessional Europe: Bureaucrats, La Bonne Police, Civilizations', in *Handbook of European History in the Late Middle Ages, Renaissance and Reformation 1400–1600*, ed. Thomas A. Brady, Heiko A. Oberman and James D. Tracey, II, Leiden 1995; id., 'Konfessionelle und politische Identität im frühneuzeitlichen Europa', in *Nationale, ethische Minderheiten und regionale Identitäten in Mittelalter und Neuzeit. Akten einer internationalen Historikerkonferenz vom 02.–04. Juni 1993 in Torun*, ed. Antoni Czacharowski, Torun 1994; id., 'Die konfessionellen Glaubenskriege und die Formierung des frühmodernen Europa', in Hans Hermann Seiler (ed.), *Glaubenskriege in Vergangenheit und Gegenwart*, Hamburg 1995 = Schriften der Joachim-Jungius-Gesellschaft E. V. der Wissenschaften Hamburg; id., 'Protestant Confessionalization in Rural Parts of Northwestern

and Northern Europe: General Considerations and Some Remarks on the Results of Case Studies', in *La christianisation des campagnes*, Proceedings of a Symposium at the University of Liège, 25–28 August 1994, ed. Jean-Pierre Massaut, Liège 1995.

2. The Reformed and mixed-confessional zone which is omitted from what follows is treated in Schilling, 'Nationale Identität (n. 1), which also discusses further examples of the formation of Catholic and Lutheran identity.

Universal Christian Faith and Nationalism

Victor Conzemius

Like the other great world religions – Buddhism, Islam and Hinduism – in theory and practice Christianity, too, makes a universal offer of salvation.[1] This universalism permeates the whole of the New Testament. Although Jesus' mission was directed first to the lost sheep of the house of Israel (Matt. 10.6; 15.24; Rom. 15.8), universalism is a constitutive element of his message. That is not only evident from Jesus' actions, for example in the encounters with the Gentile centurion (Matt. 8.5–13) or the Syro-Phoenician woman (Mark 7.24–30), but is also expressed in his message. Jesus proclaims the kingdom of God; the kingly rule of God cannot be understood in particularistic terms. God's universal will for salvation is indicated in parables. Through his merciful action the Samaritan becomes neighbour to a Jew (Luke 10.36). Jesus warns that Gentiles can sit at table in the kingdom of God together with or instead of Israel (Matt. 8.11; cf. Luke 13.28; 11.30–32). In the parable of the great banquet the servant is sent out into the highways and byways to invite guests.

Jesus maintained the election of Israel, even if Israel was not prepared to realize the role in the proclamation of the kingdom of God intended for it. Jesus' move towards outsiders, his non-observance of the dietary laws which caused separation, and later the abandonment of circumcision (Gal. 2.3), relativize the validity of the Torah. The result was a discipleship which listens to God in new ways and is open on all sides. Characteristic of this new situation is Jesus' saying about his true kin in Mark 3.35: 'Whoever does the will of my Father is my brother, and sister, and mother.'

In the description of the judgment of the world in Matt. 25 this criterion of nearness to God is expressed in a decisive way. Those who show mercy are among the 'blessed of the Father' to whom the *basileia* is promised. Without going into the problems raised by the tradition and redaction criticism of this post-Easter text, we may note that what justifies is not membership of a particular 'saving community', whether this is Israel or the church, but solely the doing of the will of God. 'What is decisive for our question is that this promise of the *basileia* has a christological foundation. Anyone who shows mercy to others is thus related to Christ, whether he himself stands inside or outside Israel. Here he is orientated on Christ, even if he does not know him.'[2]

The mission charge of the risen Christ also has a universal character (Matt.28.19). Jerusalem is the starting point of the apostles' and disciples' proclamation of their witness to Christ. Whereas in his missionary activity Paul time and again enters into discussion with Israel and warns the church of the Gentiles against arrogance (Rom. 9–11), in his speech on the Areopagus (Acts 17), Luke attempts to bring the universalism of the Christian message into harmony with the exclusiveness of salvation in Jesus Christ, without eliminating any of it. The Gentiles are in a dialectical relationship to the one true God: they do not know him, yet they worship him. The unknown God whom the Athenians worship is at the same time the true God under whose mercy all stand.

The cultural and sociological situation into which Christianity developed matched the immanent universalism of the Gospels. The Pax Romana, the relatively stable period of peace created by the Emperor Augustus, and the tolerance of the Romans, which extended as far as religious syncretism, provided ideal conditions for the extension of Christianity. The Roman empire had transformed the world into a state with a common history, with a common culture in which all had a part and to which all made an active contribution, and above all a common law, in which Roman, Greek and oriental influences were combined. The great Roman jurists of the second century humanized and universalized the small-state Roman law by adapting it to the demands of a world empire.

The gradual acceptance of Christianity after initial social scorn, periodic persecutions and literary polemic prepared for the symbiosis of the universalistic elements of Roman imperial culture with the universalism of the Christian message. We should not see this universalism as a rigid system which levelled down to uniformity the special traditions of the subject peoples. Roman imperial universalism is to be understood more as a broad-meshed conception which in the Latin West tended to encourage the spread of Christianity; whereas in the fourth century, in the West, Latin displaced Greek from the liturgy, in the lands where Christianity originated on the fringes of the empire, churches formed with their own languages and doctrinal traditions. These separated from the mainstream Latin Western and Byzantine church and were regarded as schismatic. The Syrian church, the East Syrian Nestorian church, the Indian Thomas Christians, the Coptic church and the Nubian church were all termed 'Eastern national churches'.[3]

However, this term 'national church' suggests a cohesion, purposefulness and state organization which in the full sense can be applied only to the national churches created in the nineteenth century.

We should be on our guard generally against projecting modern ideas on to the concept of the 'national'. There was no such thing as nationalism in the real sense before the eighteenth century; then, however, nationalism became the dominant ideology of the century, which also governed the understanding of history and created new myths to legitimate itself which it projected on to the past. History was identified with national history; the task of research seemed to be to investigate the development of one's own nation from its tribal and feudal origins to the realization of its own glorious statehood and to relate this history in a way which transformed it to one's advantage.[4]

National Socialism developed a particularly crude late crop of 'national' historiography. In their account of the adoption of Christianity by the Germans the National Socialist ideologues presented this as a fall which corrupted the natural characteristics of these peoples and linked them to a Jew who died on the cross.

At first there was no such threat. For where the Christian missionaries succeeded in convincing the tribal rulers of the superiority of the Christian God (e.g. the baptism of Clovis, and the conversion of the Visigothic King Reccared from Arianism), the feudal system also resulted in the conversion of the whole tribe to Christianity. Christianity replaced the tribal myths of gods fighting against one another, the notions of the divine descent of tribal kings, the worship of rivers, forests and mountains, the powerful fates, with a universal idea of God. God, the Father and Creator of all things, had communicated himself to the world by his Son Jesus Christ and had liberated humankind from all blind fate, including death itself. Christianity also attracted the Germanic peoples by its notion of a community, the church, which transcended clan, tribe and territory.

While Christianity gave the Germanic peoples a meaningful interpretation of existence, a framework within which they could set the mysteries of human life, it did not help them to create structures which corresponded to this social life of the tribe against the background of the church's universal offer of salvation. Here again a warning needs to be issued against projecting the organizational forms of modern Western Christianity, whether Roman Catholic or Protestant, on to Germanic Christianity. Despite the papacy and the episcopal church structure the Western church had a looser organizational framework, closer, say, to that of the present Orthodox churches.

Germanic Christianity was concerned neither to reform social institutions nor to increase an abstract church power. Rather, this Christianity was concerned as far as possible to secure access to the promise of heaven and guarantees against eternal damnation. Apart from monasticism the church as an organization was almost completely integrated into the social and political life of society. 'It did not stand over against political society but within it.'[5] The Germanic rulers remained *de facto* supreme religious heads of their peoples; they nominated bishops and decided liturgical and other matters. The church was completely a client church, entangled in the corruption and cruel power struggles which were so characteristic of these centuries (fifth to tenth). For the Christianization of the Germanic tribes was matched by the Germanization of Christianity, with the inevitable compromises attached to an inculturation. Only in a long-drawn-out process were legal and social conditions permeated, step by step, by Christian thinking; the biblical universalism remained an unattained postulate.

The Latin church of the West was not alone in its missionary activity. In the ninth century Byzantine Christianity began to expand. It had come up against obstacles on its eastern flank as a result of the separation of the non-Chalcedonians and the advance of Islam, and in the West encountered the barriers of a growing alienation from Rome, in a dramatic and unforeseen way. In 863 Patriarch Photius sent the brothers Cyril and Methodius to Moravia to preach the gospel there. The brothers took with them the Slavonic translation which they had made of the Bible and the liturgical books – a new development in the history of mission. In contrast to the Western church, which maintained the exclusive use of Latin as a liturgical language, the Byzantine missionaries used the vernacular of the people to whom they were preaching. This encouraged the formation among the Slavs of 'autocephalous' churches with a marked national identity. Bulgaria, Serbia and Russia adopted this form of church organization.

Not only did autocephaly become the characteristic of the church structures of the countries; they also took over from Byzantium the doctrine of the symphony of church and state. In the Byzantine political order, emperor and patriarch formed an 'organic body'. However, theory and praxis diverged considerably; in practice the emperor as 'God's image and representative' interfered massively in church affairs and in practice ruled the church. The helplessness of Orthodox churches against state involvement through the period of the Tsars, the Communist regime and the post-Communist states which have followed has one of its roots here. The identification of religion and nation which is still propagated by the church in Greece today, in the age of the European union, goes back to this ideal conception of the symphony of church and state which is incomprehensible to the Western observer.

By contrast, in the West the doctrine of two kingdoms developed by Augustine after the fall of Rome prevailed. The Cluniac reform movement and the Reform papacy of the eleventh century made a decisive contribution to it. The catalyst was the dependence of church office-holders on kings and feudal lords, which was felt to be abhorrent; in a militant and aggressive way Gregory VII enforced the distinction between spiritual and secular by his exaggerated claims and in so doing created the presuppositions for the autonomy of the modern state.[6] This process can be described as the 'first Western revolution' and the result of peaceful secularization: the hope that under papal supervision the tense relationship between emperor and pope could be regulated in a way compatible with Christian humanism was fulfilled only for a time. For a while it seemed as if Innocent III (1198–1216) could establish the universalism which was a feature of Christianity in the role of arbitrator in the tensions and clashes of interest between the Christian states; even the church was not immune to the abuse of power. In the long run the dynamic proved stronger of those powers which the church had helped to become independent: the development of a secular law and chancery with a view to a more uniform administration. This process came about through further stages of conflict between the ruler and the Pope (Philip the Fair, the Avignon schism, the late mediaeval councils, Humanism and the Reformation).

We need to note that the line of development towards nation states first remained fully within a universal Christian framework. The Reformation maintained this universalism, even if it contributed powerfully to its dissolution. The decisive break came at the time of the Enlightenment. In essentials, two strands of nationalism developed: a German strand, whose protagonists included Herder and Hegel, and a French strand, which through nationalistic rhetoric created the nation state *par excellence*. In Napoleon I's struggle for hegemony, totalitarian features became evident which in the repulsion of French expansionism gave new impetus to nationalistic fever.

How far the trend towards forming a nation had legitimate features and corresponded to historical necessity lies outside the scope of this article and is discussed elsewhere. What proved ominous was the stylizing of nationalism as religion. However, it is incorrect to call nationalism a substitute religion, since such a term obscures the central aspect of this transfer: the transfer of the absolute character of religion, specifically Christianity, to the nation. The nation became the supreme and ultimate point of reference both for the individual and for the state as a whole. The Holy Spirit was replaced by a nationalistic feeling as the power which inspired people to their highest achievements and to the sacrifice of their blood. The disturbing thing is not the adoption of the sacral language of the church – the Marseillaise as the Te Deum – or the transformation of church rites for the cultic needs of a new lay society, but the elevation of the throne of the nation to the throne of God which had become vacant.[7] The nation is the last and irrefutable authority. Christian universalism, which had also always stood under God's judgment, was displaced by the sacred egotism of the nation state. Consistently, the detachment from any link with transcendence led through the imperialistic rivalries to the genocidal catastrophe of the First World War and a short time later through the radical contempt of Christian universalism to totalitarian National Socialism.

There is some irony in the fact that Christians collaborated actively, if not in the dethronement of God, at least in the confusion of religious feeling.[8] The young Friedrich Nietzsche lamented movingly in his own – Protestant – sphere about this helpless prostitution of Christians to the idols of nationalism. It may be the case that in Protestant Germany the way from the confession to nationalism was shorter than in Catholicism.[9] The traumatic experiences of French Catholicism with a national church imposed by the state which collapsed completely within three years (1792–1795) and the serious charge of Ultramontanism made against German Catholics (suggesting that their bond with Rome was an unworthy betrayal of the national cause) dampened the readiness of Catholics to identify uncritically with the nationalist cause. But they did not remain immune. Despite the stain of Ultramontanism and the Kulturkampf, at the end of the nineteenth century the German Catholics came to terms with the Wilhelmine policy of rearmament. They were ready when in 1914 the Kaiser proclaimed this version of national universalism, to the effect that he no longer recognized any parties, but only Germans.

Although they were largely excluded in the Second Republic, and despite the separation of church and state in 1906, in 1914 the French Catholics expressed th(readiness to accept sacrificial death in battle against Luther's desce ͺnts in an exemplary way; here they were taken at their word. In 1915 the alienation of German and French Catholics reached a climax when leading French intellectuals accused the Germans of barbarism and war crimes and the Germans issued a document in reply. Finally, in 1917 the French preacher A. N. Sertillanges OP rejected the peace initiative of Pope Benedict XV with the words, 'Holy Father, we do not need your peace.'[10]

From a theological perspective, the practical capitulation of Christians to the consequences of nationalism and the *de facto* abandonment of Christian universalism in the First World War are to be attributed to the working of the mystery of evil in the church itself. However, such a remark runs the risk of removing it from rational analysis. In the specific context of modern developments in general a reference should be made to the marginalization of Christianity, the lack of suitable structures for effectuating a universalism transcending nation and race, and the difficulty of imposing its postulates, if need be with sanctions. Because of their tie to the state the Orthodox churches are not in a position to do this; only prophetic individuals can stand out here. In the nineteenth century the Patriarch of Constantinople saw himself as an advocate of Hellenism and suppressed the independence of the churches of Serbia, Roumania and above all Bulgaria, making use of excommunication. The modern papacy was in the best position to restrain an overflowing nationalism within the church.[11] In 1926, Pope Pius XI did not hesitate to condemn the integralist nationalism of Action Française,[12] as his successor, Pius XII, condemned the racism of National Socialism. However, these warnings could be effective only where the word of the Pope carried some weight and a critical distance from the tendencies of the time had been preserved in the local churches.

Translated by John Bowden

Notes

1. For the churches and nationalism see my 'Eglises et nationalismes en Europe au XIXe et XXe siècle', in A. Langner (ed.), *Europa: fondamenti, formazione e realtà*, Studi di storia moderna e contemporanea 15, Rome 1984, 269–314; *Die Kirchen und der Nationalismus. Das neue Europa. Herausforderungen für Kirche und Theologie*, Quaestiones Disputatae 144, Freiburg 1993.

2. These remarks are based on G. Lohfink, *Universalität und Exclusivität des Heils im Neuen Testament*, Quaestiones Disputatae 79, Freiburg 1977, 63–82, and O. Betz, 'Mission', *TRE* 23, 23–31.

3. C. Detlef-G. Müller, *Geschichte der orientalischen Nationalkirchen*, Die Kirche in ihrer Geschichte, 1 D2, Göttingen 1981.

4. Harold J. Berman, *Law and Revolution. The Formation of the Western Legal Tradition*, Cambridge, Mass 1983.

5. Ibid.

6. Franz Xaver Kaufmann, *Das janusköpfige Publikum von Kirche und Theologie*, Quaestiones Disputatae 144, Freiburg 1993, 11–41, esp. 26ff.

7. Here I would refer to earlier American research, especially to that of Carlton J. Hayes, who saw these wider connections at the time of the threat from modern totalitarianisms better than German scholarship of the inter-war period, which was predominantly sociological: C. J. H. Hayes, *Essays on Nationalism*, New York 1926; id., *The Historical Evolution of Modern Nationalism*, New York 1931, reissued 1963; B. C. Shafer, *Nationalism: Interpreters and Interpretations*, Washington 1959, ²1963; Emil Kauder, 'The Holy Ghost and the National Spirit. A Study in Secularization', *Virginia Quarterly Review* 26, 1950, 44–50.

8. For German Catholicism see Langner (ed.), *Europa: fondamenti, formazione e realtà* (n.1), and for Germany G. Besier, *Religion – Nation – Kultur. Die Geschichte der christlichen Kirchen in den gesellschaftlichen Umbrüchen des 19. Jahrhunderts*, Neukirchen-Vluyn 1992; also the articles by Kurt Nowak and Friedrich Wilhelm Graf in *Europa fordert die Christen. Zur Problematik von Nation und Konfession*, Regensburg 1993.

9. I stand by this remark despite some parallels to Protestant developments in the Catholic sphere; Protestantism played a pioneer role. The capitulation of the Catholics in Germany to nationalism began later.

10. Nadine Josette Chaline (ed.), *Chrétiens dans la première guerre mondiale*, Paris 1993.

11. Christiane Alix de Montclos, *Le Saint Siège et les nationalismes en Europe, 1870–1960*, Paris 1962.

12. Michael Sutton, *Charles Maurras et les Catholiques français 1890–1914. Nationalisme et positivisme*, Paris 1994.

Secularization and Nationalism

Miklós Tomka

Theories of modernization and secularization describe world history as a process of ongoing rationalization and 'disenchantment'. This is said to be an irreversible development which runs in a straight line.[1] Religion, ideologies, values are to be replaced by pragmatism and objective rationality. Quite a few authors think that they can assert the historical necessity of de-Christianization and more generally of the disappearance of religion. Others merely regard the 'privatization' of religion, its gradual suppression and withdrawal from the public sphere of society, as a natural law. Here communal and political matters are to be value-free. The liberation of their objective logic is to increase their functional effectiveness. The same tendency is supposed to result in the disappearance of the national and specifically of nationalisms.[2] However, more recent history does not seem to correspond to these expectations.

It is questionable whether history can be adequately described as a transition from value rationality to objective rationality. Rather, it involves the development of partial autonomies in individual areas of life, which always compete with other spheres in their claim to validity. History in this sense is a balancing act between human aims on the one hand and the autonomy of various partial spheres of life on the other – under the conditions of technological and socio-economic development, i.e. in constantly changing circumstances.[3] The increasing complexity tests every conscious attempt at direction orientated on values which serves human aims and interests. However, the desire to implement one's own ideas, shaped by specific preferences of values, is in no way done away with.

Differentiation destroys social and also international consensuses, the unity of aims and values. Group interests continue to exist. What becomes problematical is not the existence of individual positions based on values but whether there is any common denomination for society or for international co-existence. The process which concerns us runs through four stages. These are: 1. the unity of sacred and profane, of religion and politics, of state and church; 2. the origin of a division of work between cross and sword, between religious and profane power and rule; 3. the period of the splintering of religious unity and the formation of a new principle of organization and order, the nation; and 4. the period of ideological pluralism and an at least partial de-Christianization, when religion can be claimed on behalf of national and group interests but is hardly able to be the foundation for a unity which reconciles the conflicting parties or binds them together.

It is still an open question whether we can also speak of a fifth stage. There may be a basis for this in the insight that any resolution of conflict presupposes a dialogue, and thus a certain reciprocal acceptance of the opponents. However, the process of differentiation destroys contextual common features and links. The reification of the social world produces division and distinction, and not union. The creation of the trust needed for understanding cannot usually be expected from those immediately involved. But as institutional vehicles of the values of humanity and human determinations, the religions (and the churches, and their representatives) cannot be arbitrators; they can only offer reminders of fundamental human values. In their international responsibility for all individuals and groups they can offer themselves as places where the conflicting parties can meet. Beginnings in this direction are among the surprising events of our time and are worth special attention.

I A sacral nation?

Analyses of former cultures and of the Middle Ages often speak of sacral rule, of sacral rulers, of sacral nations.[4] Over the longest period of human history things cannot have been otherwise: there was only one, God-given, cosmic order which was established generally, and therefore also in society and in political institutions. The ruler could only be a representative. Supreme legitimation and destiny could only be derived from this order. Power could not be its own basis. The cosmic (religious) order became the aim, the criterion, the over-arching frame of reference for the socio-political system. *Polis*, society, 'nation' had this so to speak as their foundation. Here political organization did not just serve its own ends, but in principle was there to realize the divine plans. The ruler was called by God; the people was chosen by God. Purposes were seen as given by providence. The consequences of public action, too, emerged primarily in God's support or punishment.[5]

The political community at this time could be called 'nation'. Even then there could be a sense of cohesion in the political community. But this commonwealth had little to do with nations today. The integration of the pre-Christian kingdoms proved to be the result of the capacities and power of the rulers. Accordingly these kingdoms were changeable. Their frontiers were not unassailable dividing lines. Cities and areas of land could be pledged, sold, donated and so on. Whether a country spoke one language or several was unimportant. The ethnic, linguistic and often religious multiplicity did not affect the unity of the social organization. The 'nation' (in so far as we want to use this term at all here) was theoretically defined by sacral leadership, in practice through its ruler, the ruling class and its constitution. These were regarded as the instruments of divine destiny. In addition individuals and their totality as a people (but not as an autonomous nation of its own making) were incorporated into the all-embracing world order. One's own state and culture (and even one's own gods) could be claimed to be superior to the 'barbarians', the 'unbelievers' or simply the uncivilized. Here characteristics of the system but not of the people and certainly not yet of an ethnic community were being celebrated. There was no room in this world for a nationalism in the modern sense.

The unbroken unity of sacral and profane characterized the constitution of the pre-Christian kingdoms, as later it also characterized the non-European kingdoms down to the Japanese monarchy before 1945 and still characterizes some Islamic countries at present. Even in Christian Europe this unity dissolved only gradually. It left behind abiding traces. For Christianity, too, incorporation into the divine plans and order was also a special mark of legitimation.[6] Nevertheless, with the 'Christian era' the autonomy of the political order from the religious order begins.

II The balance between the religious and the profane

The historical innovation of Christianity lies in the separation of the profane from the sacral. God was known as the wholly other, omnipotent God. Through the incarnate God the total worldliness of the world could be perceived and assumed. Starting in principle from this point, it was possible to liberate the world and give it autonomy, a process which in the investiture dispute led to visible structural change. The new development consisted not only in the separation of church and state, of the sacral and the profane, but even more in the creation of a balanced combination of the two spheres. The real cultural achievement was not just the differentiation of two parts which had become independent, but the shaping of a regulated relationship between them.

This development coincides in time with the formation of the European states.[7] Christian states developed which were also independent political formations. Their constitution followed geographical, power-political, family and other factors, but hardly ethnic factors. Even where newly arrived ethically homogeneous peoples founded new kingdoms, a linguistic and ethnic mixing of the indigenous populations with the conquerors, or new settlers, began. The assimilation also embraced later waves of immigrations, as in Britain or in Central Europe. Latin as the language of administration, education and the church guaranteed international communication. Cities, craftsmen and trade used several languages. By contrast, for the scattered country population, wide political affiliations were hardly of any importance. For centuries change of abode and even native land and the consequent mixing of populations was a frequent experience for some strata: for the militant nobility, for craftsmen and artists, but also for peasant colonists. A further mixing followed as a result of the missionizing of pagan peoples and the spread of the religious orders. For a millennium Europe was not free of war and conflict, but it was international.

In this Europe, often only the nobility were counted as the nation. But it was the aristocracy who had relatives and possessions which crossed all frontiers. Nevertheless, the word nation had a meaning of its own, namely that of a political community which shared a destiny in accordance with given geographical economic and other conditions within a feudal state. 'Nation' denotes belonging to a kingdom, regardless of language or ethnic origin. This belonging only slowly became concentrated as a characteristic of differentiation. Specific, 'national' (if one likes to call them that), high cultures and popular cultures began to crystallize only gradually. The differences in political, economic and technical developments and also the clashes between the interests of different countries and regions took time to develop. However, kingdoms and 'nationes' understood themselves as parts of the Christian world and as vehicles of Christian culture, with more similarities than differences. This cohesion was reinforced by international comparisons: in the wars against the onslaught of the migrations, in the battles against the advance of Islam and in the experience of exotic lands by discoverers and merchants.

The churches were autonomous by comparison with the political structures of this time; they understood themselves as the expression of the will of God for an ordered commonwealth. The preservation of this order and the fulfilment of the duties which it had to perform could equally be interpreted as God-given obligations. Thus the rulers, government and even the people retained an aura (perhaps a quite considerable aura) of sacrality. This did not lack a function, but helped to support the sacrifices which defence of the holy order required. The solemnity of a Joan of Arc is significant in this respect, as is the literature of central and south Eastern European peoples from the period of the Turkish wars.[8] Obvious though the self-interest may have been in efforts at defence, there was an emphasis on the battle for Christianity and for Christendom. Patriotism could swell up high in word and deed. However, this was not a nationalism in the sense of a popular or ethnic effort at emancipation, a sense of superiority, a claim to rule. The balance between profane political and religious order was maintained. Christian internationalism kept special interests within bounds. A real nationalism was alien to pre-Reformation Europe.

III The cradle of nationalism

The old equilibria collapsed in modern times. The political and economic balance shifted.[9] The *una sancta catholica* split into a Roman church and an increasing number of Protestant churches. After many centuries confession and politics made new alliances.[10] Differences of confession sparked off wars. The secular power supported or opposed religious convictions. Religion became a political battle-cry. Europe, once a unity, became a mosaic of spheres of rules defined confessionally. However, religion provided only the label; the power lay in secular hands. *Cuius regio, eius religio*: the local ruler was to decide.

The crumbling of unity made self-definition necessary – above all of the new rulers and lands, but ultimately of all of them; it created pressures to prove legitimation and necessitated a religious foundation of and blessing for one's political position. Pressure arose from within to produce an ideology of one's independence and own superiority.[11] This pressure increased in the rivalry with other groups, peoples or states.

Decades or – especially in Eastern Central Europe – centuries of war created emergencies, social and political differences, hostilities and feelings of deprivation. Such feelings could develop especially around religious convictions and that style of religion which is advocated uncompromisingly by its representatives and repudiated and fought against just as uncompromisingly by its opponents.[12] The tone of the religious controversies and polemics of that time is evidence enough of the crudeness of style. And to authentic missionary zeal was added an opportunity to enlarge one's political sphere of interest on the pretext of proclaiming the faith. Persecution and the will to survive, or conversely a position of power and the feeling of being strong enough to impose one's own convictions on others, led to almost the same reactions. One's own followers must at all events be strengthened, one's own culture be shown to be superior, one's own fight proved to be a just one. People were compelled to seek those of like mind. In this confrontation on all sides, each could feel challenged and detect a compulsion towards self-assertion.

It was not individuals but parts of a group which were oppressed by the superiority of another group. Their cultural character, their confession, language and tradition were endangered. The confession was often the dividing line between groups. However, the confessional characteristics corresponded to different social and cultural needs. The successive thrusts of the Reformation gained a foothold in different groups of peoples to different extents. The religious differentiation followed a social and cultural difference which was already present. An interplay between these two factors made it possible to draw dividing lines, offered criteria and terms to denote differences, introduced the theoretical basis of separations and – through confessional intolerance – contributed to the additional alienation and hostility of regions and groups of the population.

One special factor which must not be neglected is the link between religion and the political system.[13] This took its clearest and most abiding form in the Protestant state churches. However, 'Catholic' monarchies or the political role of the religious orders also provided instances on the non-Protestant side. The politicization of a religion in a sphere of rule had similar consequences in groups which were political opponents, usually concerning other religions. Soon confessions were celebrated as 'national' religions in order to produce awareness of the coincidences of national and confessional persecution, or even to provoke resistance.

The Reformation or the religious splintering of Europe, part of the more comprehensive process of this political coming of age, also contributed to national development and differentiation and to the formation of a national feeling and nationalism. From then on it was above all the churches, as powerful cultural organizations, which gave protection to the tender plants of the 'national' and nationalism (as also for nations newly coming into being) and helped them to grow. With the Reformation the internationalizing power of Christianity became weak. Belonging to a confession became a support for national identities. Already existing social and cultural divergencies found possibilities of expression in the churches which were dividing, indicating what they felt to be hostile and depicting their own position as in accordance with the will of God.[14] Nationalism became politically functional and acceptable in religious and moral terms.

It would be a misunderstanding to regard the Reformation or the confessional splintering of Christianity as a cause of nationalism. But these furthered the development, in which socio-political differentiation and emancipation went hand in hand.[15] It is difficult to assess this state of affairs. There is no disputing the constructive functions of nationalism in European history, as also later in the origin and liberation of the new nations of the Third World. These functions included group integration, the creative motivation of culture, the strengthening of cultural and political self-confidence, political emancipation, and so on.[16] However, it must be asked whether these functions can outbalance the destructive potential of nationalism. The answer may differ from case to case and depend on perspective.

IV Nationalism as substitute religion?

The most recent period has led to an unprecedented situation. Modern societies are characterized by their pluralism and by the volatilization of the consensus over values.[17] Those who have religious commitments to a church are only a minority. The majority resort to a religion they have put together themselves or are uninterested in religion. Basic values are under discussion. It is a disputed question how a society can function without an identifiable cultural basis. At any rate it seems less capable of leading its citizens to great common efforts. But political independence newly entered into, or the acceleration of economic development, can require such efforts.[18] The sudden mobilization of people occasionally needs 'pre-modern' means and strategies, like compulsion or force, without fanatical visions of the future. The twentieth century is the century of dictatorships and doctrines of salvation in this world.[19] But what is left after the fiascos of ideologies on both the right and left wings?

Today there are no fewer common ethical and national features and self-interests than there were before. And there is no sign that the international community of states has sure ways of resolving the sharp clashes of interest. Bitterness against imagined or actual disadvantages is piling up in many places.[20] Many nations, especially the smaller ones which are perhaps stateless, can easily find themselves in a situation where they are anxious for their identity or their existence. The battle for survival can spark off nationalism and – at least in the eyes of those involved – even legitimate it.

The excessive emphasis on a national right to exist and national interests may have its roots in popular crises. But the mobilizing force of ethnic and national argument develops in other ways. The nation is a factor which can be identified and to some degree grasped. One's own involvement in it is clear. The nation offers itself as the dominant institution for formulating cultural identities and as a vehicle for implementing both individual and group interests. It can easily become the most general form of feeling of 'us'. 'Outside' the nations are 'the others', the competition, the threat, perhaps the enemies. Now that traditional religions have become unsure, this profane system of reference can take on totalitarian, quasi-religious characteristics. At all events it is a likely starting point for ideologies with a claim to absoluteness. Is this a perverse development? It is more an emergency situation to guarantee a framework for the integration of the group, the people of the state, the linguistic community or whatever, when there is no religious or cosmic reference. Nationalism creates its own sacred microcosm from within, in a way which cannot be refuted from outside.

V Religious corrections to nationalism?

The pluralism of modernity and the 'disenchantment' of the world are unchangeable facts. In these conditions no religion can produce and guarantee a seamless social unity for the whole of society, or even for larger regions. Yet religion seems to have the capacity to overcome nationalistic and other group egotism in two respects. Base communities and spiritual movements in the mainstream churches are forming beyond national, ethnic and linguistic boundaries, like the new communities of the sects and the new religious movements. Religious conversion, illumination and the experience of community communicate both a relationship to God and an openness to fellow human beings. In the everyday life of many religious communities a practice of reconciliation and all-embracing solidarity is set over against nationalism.[21] 'There is neither Jew nor Greek' (Gal. 3.28), nor other bitter enmities – that is what religious groups are still experiencing today. These are living proofs that nationalism can be overcome. Their starting point, faith, cannot be transferred by this model at random, nor to the whole of society. But is more to be expected from religion in modern society?

The most spectacular developments of religious change in modernity include a shift in social function. The growth of individualism limits the power of institutional religion to regulate private matters. But it gains importance in another sphere.[22] This increasingly complex world, branching in so many varied directions and becoming so differentiated, has a functional need for impartial mediators, for institutions for dialogue, for a reference to its shared cultural roots.[23] There is a lack of such institutions. Perhaps that is the explanation why religion and churches are again increasingly being recognized as political authorities with international relevance. However, they cannot overcome nationalism. Still, they can set in motion dialogues which will help towards understanding. And in every country they can further the recognition of the concerns of other countries and nations. In this way they can open the way towards taking the edge off nationalism.

Translated by John Bowden

Notes

1. Of course this covers only one strand in the theories of secularization, cf. K. Dobbelaere, 'Secularization, a Multi-Dimensional Concept', *Current Sociology* 29, 1981, 1–213; H. Lubbe, *Säkularisierung. Geschichte eines ideenpolitischen Begriffs*, Freiburg and Munich 1965.

2. T. Parming and C. L. Mee-Yau, 'Modernization and Ethnicity', in J. Dofny and A. Akiwowo (eds.), *National and Ethnic Movements*, Beverley Hills and London 1980, 131–42.

3. W. Schluchter, *Rationalismus der Weltbeherrschung*, Frankfurt 1980.

4. For classics on the questions of charismatic leadership see M. Weber, *Economy and Society* (1921), Berkeley 1979; for sacral legitimation cf. id., *Gesammelte Aufsätze zur Religionssoziologie* I–III, Tübingen 1920. Cf. also B. Gladigow (ed.), *Staat und Religion*, Düsseldorf 1981.

5. For the logic of this unity from different perspectives, cf. P. L. Berger, *The Sacred Canopy*, Garden City 1967, and W. Stark, *The Sociology of Religion*, I, *Established Religion*, New York 1966.

6. P. Brown, *The World of Late Antiquity*, London 1971.

7. H. Pirenne, *Histoire économique et sociale du Moyen Age*, Paris 1969, and R. W. Southern, *Western Society and the Church in the Middle Ages*, Harmondsworth 1978.

8. Stark, *Sociology of Religion* I (n.5).

9. B. Giesen (ed.), *Nationale und kulturelle Identität*, Frankfurt 1991.

10. H. Schilling, 'Nationale Identität und Konfession in der europäischen Neuzeit', in ibid., 192–252.

11. E. Gellner, *Nations and Nationalism*, Oxford 1983, 40f.

12. We should not forget the introduction of the vernacular into the liturgy, the translations of the Bible, and the new technique of book printing, which similarly encouraged the vernacular. Cf. H. Kohn, *Nationalism*, Princeton 1955.

13. W. Stark, *The Sociology of Religion, III, The Universal Church,* New York 1967.

14. Gellner, *Nations and Nationalism* (n.11), 71f.

15. Weber's Protestantism thesis (*The Protestant Ethic and the Spirit of Capitalism* [1904/6], London 1985) sparked off a discussion on the role of the Reformation as a catalyst which is still going on today. From the earliest contributions cf. R. H. Tawney, *Religion and the Rise of Capitalism*, London 1926.

16. Dofny and Akiwowo (eds.), *National and Ethnic Movements* (n.2), and H. Mol (ed.), *Identity and Religion*, London 1971; R. Mitchison (ed.), *The Roots of Nationalism. Studies in Northern Europe*, Edinburgh 1980.

17. From a historical perspective cf. H. McLeod, *Religion and the People of Western Europe 1789–1970*, Oxford 1981. For a cultural comparison cf. D. Lerner, *The Passing of Traditional Society*, New York and London 1958. For the sociological aspect cf. P. L. Berger and B. Berger, *The Homeless Mind: Modernization and Consciousness*, New York 1973, and H. v. d. Loo and W. v. Rijen, *Modernisierung*, Munich 1992.

18. Gellner speaks of social entropy and its control by nationalism, *Nations and Nationalism* (n.11), 63ff.

19. H. L. Featherstone reckons the age of nationalism as beginning in 1815. Cf. *A Century of Nationalism*, London 1939.

20. Cf. e.g. F. Fanon, *The Wretched of the Earth*, Harmondsworth 1967.

21. J.-T. Maertens, *Les petits groupes et l'avenir de l'Église*, Paris 1971; D. Marti, *Tongues of Fire*, Oxford 1990; J. O'Halloran, *Signs of Hope: Developing Small Christian Communities*, Maryknoll 1991; J. P. Pinto, *Inculturation through Basic Communities*, Bangalore 1985; B. Uguex, *Les petites communautés chrétiennes*, Paris 1988.

22. P. E. Hammond (ed.), *The Sacred in a Secular Age*, Berkeley, Los Angeles and London 1985; H. J. Höhn. *Gegen/Mythen. Religionsproduktive Tendenzen der Gegenwart*, Freiburg 1994; R. Robertson, *Globalization*, London, Newbury Park and New Delhi 1992; R. Withnow, *Rediscovering the Sacred: Perspectives on Religion in Contemporary Society*, Grand Rapids 1992.

23. M. Featherstone (ed.), *Global Culture. Nationalism, Globalization and Modernity*, London, Newbury Park and New Delhi 1990.

II · Patriotism, Nationalism and the Duties of Citizens

Patriotism and Nationalism

Heinrich Schneider

I

Patriotism, commonly identified with love of one's country, has long been regarded even in Christian thought as a duty and at the same time as a virtue. The Second Vatican Council exhorts citizens to cultivate love of their country 'with pride and loyalty'; 'love of nation' is commended to Catholics, as is performing the duties of a citizen.[1] It is a teaching which goes far back into tradition that this duty to love one's country even includes readiness to sacrifice one's own life.[2]

On the other hand, the church's magisterium has unmistakably warned against nationalism which gives the appearance of *caritas patriae* but in truth is *cupiditas intemperantiae* (in modern language 'power-hungry imperialism'),[3] which destroys the *fundamenta* of the *res publica*[4] and is an enemy of true peace and prosperity.[5]

In other words, patriotism is a good thing and nationalism a bad thing. But what is the difference between the two?

There is a common answer to this question: the difference is one of degree; it consists as it were in a difference of temperature – healthy patriotism has a good temperature, and nationalism is overheated patriotism. This is an inadequate view, in which qualitative criteria are overlooked or deliberately omitted. We need to investigate it.

II

Patriotism is a traditional affair. In Christian tradition love of one's country is seen as a duty and at the same time as a virtue, but here love of one's heavenly country has priority over love of one's earthly country.[6]

What is special about this love of one's earthly country, as it is seen in church tradition, emerges from the vocabulary that we find in the conciliar texts mentioned above. Both texts talk of *pietas*. The Latin term primarily means an observance which is a matter of duty[7] and – put emphatically – reverential submission to and concern for parents. It is that attitude of which the fourth commandment of the Decalogue speaks, but *pietas* is to be shown not only to parents but also to other relations and especially to the *patria*, the earthly commonwealth, the land, the cultural environment to which one owes the possibility of one's own development – and the gods. However, in ancient Rome *pietas* – one of the fundamental values of the Roman way of life – was an attitude involving mutual concern: there was also a *pietas* which the *pater familias* showed to his family, and one which human beings might expect of the gods.[8] The ancient Romans saw this virtue embodied in the most evocative way in Virgil's *Aeneid*: Virgil shows and proves his *pietas* not only to his father, his wife, his son and his followers but also to the gods and to his *patria*, old and new; indeed even to the vicissitudes of his fate.[9]

However, in the history of the term there are also some special emphases which are by no means obvious to us today: it is worth mentioning at least some of them.

– In antiquity, for the Greeks the word which corresponded to the Latin *pietas* was *eusebeia*; it too is due to gods and men and also to the *polis*, the civic community in which one lives, to which one has obligations and which is itself under divine protection.[10] By contrast, for the ancient Greeks *patriotes* is an expression related to descent, to membership of a community, which is used of someone who has no *politeuma* and is no citizen of a *polis*; the term is also used to denote the origin of slaves or wild animals.[11] The 'patriotic' belongs so to speak in the lower sphere of necessity, not in the higher sphere of freedom and virtue.

– That also corresponds to the Roman view: 'It is not the fatherland which is worthy of the Roman citizen's devotion, perhaps his sacrifice, but the *res publica*, the common interests of the people . . .'[12] Really *pietas* is due, alongside the gods, to ancestors and kin, and in the Roman view also to the political commonwealth.[13] Down to the time of Cicero, *patria* is really a shorthand term for *patria urbs*.[14]

For ancient Greek thought, too, the world around, the homeland, as it were the inner nucleus of the 'fatherland', is primarily a combination of cultural attitudes, the binding quality of which is comprehensively crystallized out in the order of the *polis*.[15]

– When we come to the mediaeval understanding, for Thomas Aquinas, *pietas* is on the one hand a social virtue and on the other a gift of the Holy

Spirit; in the last sense it is the piety, that inner attitude, which gives joyfully and trustingly to God what is God's, the fruits of which are *bonitas* and *benignitas*.[16] By contrast, the human virtue of *pietas* is directed towards God, towards parents and blood relations, and towards the *patria* (the 'fatherland'). Thomas justifies this by pointing out that we owe our being most of all to God – God is the first primal ground of all reality and especially of every human soul – and then to our parents, and finally to our *patria*, the place or land or space where we have received from the world before and around us what has made it possible for us to flourish; precisely for that reason the *patria* is part of the 'ground of our being'.[17]

Since, then, we have received benefits from God the creator, from our parents and our family and from our fellow-citizens (namely, those which make our own existence possible and meaningful), and to this degree are in their debt, we should respond to them with our respectful *pietas*: this is a command of righteousness.[18]

In ancient tradition it is even said that the *patria* is due more devotion than parents.[19]

Thomas does not explain the term *patria* itself; he presupposes it without clearly having in mind the sense of *polis* characteristic of the ancient Greeks or the republican dimension of Roman *pietas*.[20] But he has in view the primarily cultural and spiritual content of *patria*: this is not something spatial or topographical but the world around, society, the *communicationes concivium*. All fellow citizens (*omnes concives*) belong to the *patria*, in the main part indeed they make it up; the *pietas* due to the *patria* moreover includes all those who are bound up in solidarity with the *patria*.[21]

– In modern times 'patriotism' then takes on another colouring:[22] Leibniz sees the characteristic of the true patriot in the love of his fatherland and a consequent concern to further its well-being; in England patriotism is identified with public spirit, in France with commitment to the common good, the public interest. But then, especially in the thought of the French Revolution, the meaning of the term goes over into the sphere of republican nationalist thinking. For Rousseau, 'patriotisme' is obligation to the 'volonté générale'. In his understanding of patriotism, Kant endeavours to reconcile the traditional notion of piety towards the fatherland which we have found in Thomas Aquinas (though now without any reference to the metaphysic of principles of being) with the republican civic freedom and civic virtue.[23] Soon patriotism and national consciousness become amalgamated in such a way that they seem to be the conscious identification of the individual with the nation; the original content of patriotism passes over into nationalism.

III

It is almost a commonplace that nationalism and the national sense which corresponds to it are modern phenomena as compared with the 'patriotism' of old Europe, regardless of the fact that already in antiquity there is mention of *nationes*.[24] But is there a convincing basis for this thesis? If we are to examine it, we must define clearly the content of both patriotism and nationalism. In the case of nationalism this raises difficulties. Where 'nation' and 'nationalism' are concerned, there is 'widespread agreement that one cannot find a binding and generally acceptable definition of the two terms'.[25]

Reinhart Koselleck points out that here there is 'the self-organization and self-perception of political units of action and other units of action, or alien groups which they exclude'.[26] The same thing cannot be said of patriotism: as a rule it does not constitute the *patria* – however that might be defined – but presupposes its existence. On the other hand there were and are quite other kinds of political units of action – alongside that defined as a nation: for example the *polis*, the confederation with a dynastic stamp, the trans-national state, the political commonwealth constituted and defined in political terms (from the *sacrum imperium* to the 'Islamic republic'), or even the multinational 'fatherland of the working population'. The assumption that all alternatives to the nation as the only principle of political identity are things of yesterday or the day before is inconclusive if one does not regard the nation as a so to speak metaphysical category.[27]

Whether it is, however, is disputed today. This can be demonstrated with reference to two positions, those of Bernhard Giesen on the one hand and Kurt Hübner on the other.

In present-day sociology there is a widespread view that the 'nation' is a human invention, what Bernhard Giesen thinks is 'by no means an inviolate form of collective identity', 'not given by nature . . . but the result of variable historical conditions and a social construct with various points of reference',[28] in order to justify the identity and thus the existence of particular social units.[29] Underlying this is the well-known 'Thomas theorem': 'If men define situations as real, they are real in their consequences.'[30] Not only are particular nations concrete and transitory, but the category itself must be understood in a 'nominalistic' way. The antithesis claims that the identity of a nation is a necessary condition of human social life, just as the identity of a person is indispensable for that person's flourishing (thus e.g. K. Hübner).[31] But as there is no 'empirical proof of a national identity of essence' – of the kind that 'some Romantics dreamed of'[32] – what status in reality does 'the national' have, and what claim to validity can it make? Hübner's reply is: that of 'the truth of myth';[33] the national consciousness has a 'mythical' character and a 'numinous component'.[34] However, in his view there have also been 'pseudo-myths' which have no truth, which lack 'historical regularity', have a fictitious and illusory character, have derived from a political will and serve it – and are related to true myths as pseudo-scientific ideologies are related to science.[35] But 'mythical national consciousness' does not fall under this category of pseudo-myths; it cannot be denied its 'ontological right'.[36]

Both positions, the nominalistic (as in Giesen) and the mytho-ontological (as in Hübner), conclude that it is therefore difficult to define anything like the essence of the nation. It is impossible to derive it from a combination of particular objectifiable constitutional elements like common descent, common language, common faith or whatever.

So as a rule, 'functional' characterizations of the idea of the nation, and especially nationalism, have become customary; these stop at its contribution towards solidarity and integration.[37] Thus even so great an expert as Heinrich August Winkler emphasizes that the nation should bring about the mobilization of a larger group conceived as a 'nation' against adversaries inside and outside, and justify the priority of national loyalty on the part of citizens and groups over all other loyalties. With this Winkler links the statement, 'But the nation in whose sign the integration takes place is . . . a symbol which resists being deciphered.'[38]

If that is the case, we should investigate the position; that is presumably more fruitful than ignoring it or brushing it aside with the claim that here is a myth for which there is no rational explanation.[39]

IV

If it is so diffficult to uncover the real basis (the principle, the origin) of the symbol 'the nation' – what may the reason be? When is an origin concealed? As a rule, when it is illegitimate, and that is the case here.

The modern idea of the nation is not without reason a modern one – i.e. one which only arises in connection with the Christian Middle Ages.[40] We can say quite precisely when it came into the world, in 1789. At that time Abbé Emmanuel Sieyès, in 'the most successful pamphlet of all time', entitled 'What is the Third Estate?', with revolutionary radicalism declared the nation to be the sovereign ground of politics: it 'exists before all else', it is 'the origin of all things', it is 'independent of all forms and conditions',[41] subject to no constitution, and its law is always the supreme law.[42] Sieyès the theologian gives the nation the traditional predicates of God: the identity of essence and existence, being from the beginning, the quality of the *causa prima*, omnipotence, omniscience and all goodness. One truly cannot proclaim the nation's claim to rule and loyalty more unconditionally than with these notions. They were not conceived *ex nihilo* by Sieyès; behind them lies Jean Jacques Rousseau's doctrine of the sovereignty of the people.[43] Rousseau is similarly a theologian in disguise – or a pseudo-theologian: he attributes superhuman sovereignty to the 'volonté générale'. It is not an empirical entity, although it alone can give the political order true legitimacy. Democracy, says Rousseau, is no use at all to human beings; it is the appropriate constitution for a people of gods.[44] It would have been more correct had he said 'for a divinized people'. If an empirical, real people is to have a right constitution, it needs a 'législateur', a lawgiver.[45] His task is not, say, to formulate a constitutional document; rather, as Rousseau explains, first he must so to speak transform human nature: he must replace a bodily autonomous existence with a participatory and spiritual existence – he must communicate to the people life which participates in the spirit, indeed in a superhuman spirit. This task has nothing in common with human rule: the 'législateur' does not give any order and has no earthly power (his earthly power is 'virtually nil').

That means that he has to achieve something which transcends human power; if this task is to be fulfilled it can happen only by virtue of a power which is not of this world. The constitution of the 'corps politique' puts people in a new state of existence; it represents the transformation of human nature, or, in biblical terms, the transubstantiation of the 'old Adam' into the 'new'. In Rousseau's language: the grounding of the true commonwealth, the constitution of the 'volonté générale', liberates men from being imprisoned in 'amour propre', and instils *amor boni* in them in place of 'self-seeking' (what Augustine calls *amor sui*). In Augustine this *amor boni*, this existential resolution for the good, is unmistakeably called *amor Dei*. But in a text composed some time before the *Contrat social*, Rousseau himself had recognized that God himself is the centre on which 'good' men who are not imprisoned in self-seeking are orientated – as a result of which they also come to agree among themselves and become a true society.[46] And finally the concept of 'volonté générale' – misunderstood by those ignorant of the history of ideas as a theoretical democratic construction by Rousseau – is in reality a theological term current in his time: it simply means the will of God.[47] Moreover Sieyès also refuses to use the expression, speaking instead of the 'volonté commune'.[48]

That means that the modern idea of the nation which derives from Rousseau and Sieyès is the political appropriation of a theological concept. There are comparable reinterpretations in other thinkers concerned with the nation. For example, when Johann Gottfried Herder's doctrine of the spirit of the people claims that historical reality brings to manifestation a metaphysical substance which binds the members of a people to national identity, this means that national solidarity rests on the participation of the members of the people in this metaphysical substance.[49]

Such notions did not arise by chance. Since the twelfth century the Pauline term *corpus mysticum* has been the designation for the community of those who believe in Christ, who find their common identity in the *pneuma tou Christou*, in the mystical, supernatural reality of the transfigured Christ in which they participate spiritually and in the eucharist.[50] In a culture the spirit of which is shaped by theology, because those who have the normative knowledge are theologians, any commonwealth will be understood as a variation on the origin and embodiment of all forms of comity, the church – it is so to speak the realized idea, the pattern of all social unity. Thus for example already in the thirteenth century Vincent of Beauvais used the analogy of the *corpus reipublicae mysticum* and the *corpus Christi mysticum*. On the frontier between the Middle Ages and modern times, Sir John Fortescue then understood the political community in terms of the church community: its unity rests on the participation of the members in a metaphysical substance. This can either turn into a mere figure of thought which to some extent prepares for the nominalistic constructions of social theory, or the analogy can be taken seriously in realistic terms: in that case every community is a *corpus mysticum*, whose unity lies in a metaphysical substance. This is also true of a political commonwealth; its members belong to this substance, or they appropriate it so that they live as it were from it and in it, like believing Christians in Christ. If against the background of such notions one notes that there are also other nations, then there is a temptation to elevate one's own nation above the others – say by attributing to it a saving mission for all peoples. Jakob Talon has described how this happens time and again with the use of theological concepts like 'redemption', 'resurrection', 'revelation' and 'rebirth'.[51] The work of salvation can consist in the proclamation of justice and righteousness, in the proclamation of a *nova lex*, or in the exemplary moral character of one's own nation, in analogy to the *Christos paidagogos*; the saving quality of a nation can also be expressed in a suffering and sacrifice like that of the servant of God (elements of such notions existed and still exist e.g. in Polish or Serbian nationalism).

In other words, nationalism is not some kind of ideology of the integration of major groups or a patriotism with highly emotional overtones; such attempts at interpretation bracket off the content of the national idea. If, by contrast, we take this content directly into account, we recognize that it is really a refunctioning of something else, the product of the particularization of an element of Christian faith and thus a substitute religious construct. If we see how it came to be formulated prototypically, then we will include it more among the 'pseudo-myths' than among the mythical truths.

V

So if nationalism – particularly in the Christian perspective – is a suspicious, questionable thing, how can it be overcome, and what alternatives are there? The renewal of old 'patriotism' in its ancient version or that developed by Thomas Aquinas? Or what else?

If we want to investigate this question we must first reflect on the need which nationalism – adequate or inadequate – meets.

A political community needs a force to give it unity and to preserve that unity. It is not enough for the ruling order to be regarded as legitimate, and certainly not enough that it and the decisions made within its framework should be accepted on assessments of interests and calculation. To put this in the language of contemporary political systems theory, it is not enough for the political institutions as such to be given support; they must also rest on a political community, be rooted in it, though conversely it is also the task of the political system to contribute to keeping this political community in existence.[52] The classical, Aristotelian theory of politics speaks of *philia* (*amicitia*, solidarity) as the substance of the community which makes itself felt in the spirit where there can no longer be a wider order because there are no interpersonal links between all members – Aristotle defines *philia politike* as *homonoia (concordia)*.[53] Nowadays, the problem is usually discussed under the title 'identity', e.g. national, and sometimes also European.[54] Sometimes it is developed in terms of the questions: 'Who are we? Where do we come from? Where are we going? What do we await? What awaits us?' But these questions presuppose another question: Why and how do we see ourselves in a position to, or find ourselves compelled to, speak to one another and of one another in the first person plural? Different answers to this are possible, for example because we form a 'community of culture and character' shaped by 'the common experience or suffering of fate . . .'[55] Or, because we are in the presence of the same challenges and needs – because we find ourselves in the same situation. It is the common 'definition of the situation' which unites us; in particular it can be shaped by a 'core system of shared meanings',[56] so that participation in a common world of meaning brings *concordia*.[57]

However, this community of the world of meaning and the interpretation of the situation (along with its historical depth-dimension, its perspectives on the future and the challenges and tasks perceived here) is only one of the requirements of collective identity; another is demarcation. 'All identity constitutes itself through negations',[58] and the awareness of our special tasks means that it is not a matter of just any tasks: *'nostra res agitur'*. Nothing creates and strengthens group identity so much as a common enemy, a 'wholly other' adversary; so that quite often hostile stereotypes are conjured up to stabilize identity.[59] National identity is often defined by reference to counter-identities.[60]

A third demand of fully developed collective identity is the capacity to act and the capacity for responsibility – in some way analogous to the fact that individual identity embraces not only self-identity but ego-identity. At any rate, without competence in action which includes a capacity for self-assurance, collective identity is on the way to itself. However, that calls for 'representation', representative making present, and the realization by specific persons of contents and claims which create and safeguard identities;[61] this is also called 'authorization'. Through authorization a community becomes a 'collective agent'. That means that the formation of political institutions is a constitutive and integral element of the formation of the identity of a community.[62] Political institutions also provide 'existential representation' and at the same time can be understood as forms of leading ideas and as means of a capacity for collective action.[63]

If the problem of political identity, its constitution and preservation, is to be understood appropriately, then we must consider all this in its context.

Only on this presupposition is it possible to understand appropriately the function of nationalism in creating and safeguarding identity and alternative principles of identity.

Here in particular the question arises why and in what circumstances nationalism made a breakthrough in the form characterized above.

There is one possible answer. After the widespread acceptance of the contrast between the terms 'national culture' and 'nation state' deriving from Friedrich Meinecke,[64] Theodor Schieder has developed a triadic typology of the formation of the nation state and also of the 'national or nationalistic mentalities' which go with it.[65] Nationalism first articulates itself as a political will of the previous subjects to 'take power' in an existing state. 'The nation becomes . . . a creation of revolutionary emancipation',[66] but beforehand it forms itself to fight for this. The prototype of this is the French Revolution. Secondly, nationalism develops where the overcoming of the political division of a nation is proclaimed; this is not to conquer an existing state but to create a new one: the existing multiplicity of states is felt as a suppression of unity and a hindrance to it. The corresponding nationalisms are formed, as in the cases of Germany and Italy, as movements for union or as their ideologies. Thirdly, nationalism forms, conversely, as a movement of secession in which the existing imperial state is felt to be a prison for the peoples, as has happened in Central and Eastern Europe; here it was a matter of achieving freedom from Tsarist Russian, Hapsburg or Ottoman Turkish foreign rule.[67]

In the first the political map remains as it were unchanged; in the second it loses its colour; and in the third it becomes more colourful. In other words, in the last two models the sovereignty of the nation must be established against existing state orders: the justification of the will to form a nation state therefore needs to refer to a metapolitical principle standing 'behind' or 'over' the political reality. That helps us to understand how nationalism in Central and Eastern Europe is based on the proclamation of a natural culture which has come about independently of existing states and now must be given its political rights; in the case of France, which is characteristic of Schieder's first model, the nation wants to make the existing state its state, and it is therefore clear that the existing conscience corresponds to the type of the nation state.

However, in all three cases an unconditional, national solidarity which transcends other political solidarities must be proclaimed, and a loyalty to the nation must be established in the face of all other loyalties. The previous ruling order oppresses freedom. Its claim to recognition and obedience, indeed to the divine will, is untrue and unjust. As an ordinance of a higher law, the sovereignty of the nation needs the foundation of its metaphysical or even supernatural dignity. At the time of the Enlightenment the appeal to a law of nature or reason might have been appropriate, but then it was a matter of motivating intellectual minorities.

Now religious (or pseudo-religious) slogans are being proclaimed, also because it is a matter of mobilizing many people and securing not the demolition, but the activation and use, of potential religious motives. In other words, the radicalizing of the claim of loyalty in a context of battle leads people astray into offering as it were the highest and last powers of the soul and delegitimating all thought and will that opposes them. The diabolizing of the enemy, the old, 'evil' order, and the sanctification of one's own cause match each other.

However, this suggests that only a change in the political constellation, so to speak a defusing of the conflicts over the structure of the community and the constitution of national existence, offers an opportunity for overcoming nationalism.

In favour of what political consciousness should we want this to happen?

An attempt at renewing the 'old' patriotism which bases the identity of the people and the state solely on origins – on what has been inherited from the fathers – will probably hardly do justice to the demands of the time (just as 'traditional legitimacy' as understood by Max Weber is probably also a thing of the past), far less those of the future. On the other hand solidarity – also and particularly in modern societies – can have many foundations, beginnings and references. It is impossible to go into them in this article.

Certainly what is indispensable is a constant concern for a unifying awareness of present challenges and the tasks of the community in the future, and also a positive understanding of the constituent elements of the political order which ensure loyalty, an understanding which contributes to recognition and commitment in the service of human dignity. What has recently been called 'constitutional patriotism' is not an artificially devised substitute for national consciousness which is 'really desirable', as some claim, but a legacy of the old European tradition[68] which should not be underestimated. Not least, because it does not stand in the way of the possibilities and needs of European union.[69]

Translated by John Bowden

Notes

1. *Gaudium et spes* 75: '*cives pietatem erga patriam magnanimiter et fideliter excolant*'; *Apostolicam actuositatem* 14: '*In pietate erga nationem et in fideli implet-*

ione officiorum civilium catholici obligatos se sentiant ad verum bonum commune promovendum.'

2. Cf. e.g. B. Häring, *Das Gesetz Christi*, Freiburg [7]1963, Vol. III, 171f.

3. Pius XI, *Ubi arcano* (1922).

4. Pius XI, *Caritate Christi compulsi* (1932).

5. Pius XI, *Divini illius Magistri* (1929).

6. Cf. e.g. the references to Ambrose of Milan, Augustine and John Chrysostom in Otto Schilling, *Lehrbuch der Moraltheologie* II, Munich 1928, 667f. The comparative restraint of more recent German-language accounts of 'patriotism' or 'love of fatherland' is striking.

7. Thus A. A. T. Ehrhard, *Politische Metaphysik von Solon bis Augustin*, I, Tübingen 1985, referring to W. Warde Fowler, *The Religious Experience of the Roman People*, 1912, 430f.

8. Cf. E. Burck, 'Drei Grundwerte der römische Lebensordnung (*labor-moderatio-pietas*)', in H. Oppermann (ed.), *Römertum*, Darmstadt 1962, 35ff., 60; R. Riehs, '*Pietas*', in J. Ritter and K. Gründer (eds.), *Historisches Wörterbuch der Philosophie* 7, Basel 1989, 971f.

9. Riehs, *Historisches Wörterbuch* (n.8), 971f.

10. As is well known, the accusation of having failed to show piety towards the city led to the death sentence on Socrates; that he accepted the verdict despite its injustice and despite the opportunity to flee is a demonstration of his supreme *eusebeia*.

11. H. J. Busch and U. Dierse, 'Patriotismus', in Ritter and Gründer, *Historisches Wörterbuch* (n.8), 207ff.

12. E. Meyer, *Römischer Staat und Staatsgedanke*, Zurich [2]1961, 272.

13. For Romans up to the time of Cicero, *patria* is really a shorthand term for *patria urbs*, see Meyer, *Römischer Staat* (n.12), 239. When all Italy was included in the republic, the municipal constitution was introduced for communities not belonging to the *urbs*; their political autonomy formed the basis for a distinctive civic bond: 'Every citizen now had two fatherlands (*duae patriae*), his native city and Rome' (ibid., 314.).

14. Ibid., 239.

15. 'Ethos is one's abode, and then the place of one's distinctive customs. So custom, usage, origin, ways of right and seemly behaviour and also the institutions which support these are ethical' (J. Ritter, *Metaphysik und Politik*, Frankfurt am Main 1969, 110). At the same time, Ritter points out that the expression 'ethos' originally and down to Aristotle is applied to living beings generally; so it is primarily also rooted in the realm of 'necessity' and runs into human morality only in political existence.

16. Thomas Aquinas, *STh* II.II, 121.

17. Ibid., 101,. 1 ad 3.

18. Ibid., 60, 3; cf. also ibid I.II, 60, 3: '*ad iustitiam enim pertinere videtur ut quis debitum reddat, (puta) pietas qua redditur debitum parentibus vel patriae.*'

19. See the references to passages in Augustine and Ambrose in Schilling, *Lehrbuch der Moraltheologie* (n.6), 608.

20. For the significance of *patria* in the Middle Ages cf. E. H. Kantorowicz, *The King's Two Bodies*, New York 1957.

21. Thomas Aquinas, *STh* II.II, 101, 1. Blood relatives also deserve *pietas* so to speak not by virtue of common descent but on the basis of *communicationes consanguineorum* (ibid.). The phrase used last in the text above stands for the formula *omnium patriae amicorum*, which can be read in Thomas. This is appropriate, because

amicitia corresponds to the Greek *philia*, and *philia* means solidarity and spiritual community of will: *amicitia* makes itself known in *idem velle et nolle* – thus Thomas himself, quoting Sallust, in ibid II.II 104.3. *Amicitia* is synonymous with 'solidarity' and *caritas socialis* in Pope John Paul II, encyclical *Centesimus annus* 10. For the identification of the *philia* and solidarity cf. also E. Thiemer, *Solidarität als ethischer, gesellschaftstheoretischer und politischer Begriff,* Vienna dissertation 1991.

22. The following references to the development from Leibniz to Rousseau follow Busch and Dierse, 'Patriotismus' (n.11).

23. He calls patriotism 'the manner of thinking in which each person in the state (not excluding its supreme head) regards the commonwealth as the mother's womb or the fatherland from and in which he himself arose, only in order to protect its rights by laws of the common will, and does not think it legitimate to subject it to his own unconditional preference to use.' Thus I. Kant, 'Über den Gemeinspruch: Das mag in der Theorie richtig sein, taugt aber nicht für die Praxis', in *Werke*, ed. W. Weischedel, 9, Darmstadt 1968, 127ff.: 146.

24. For the topic cf. H. O. Ziegler, *Die moderne Nation*, Tübingen 1931; K. Renner, *Die Nation: Mythos und Wirklichkeit* (1937), Vienna 1964; H. Kohn, *The Idea of Nationalism*, New York 1944; W. Sulzbach, *Imperialismus und Nationalbewusstsein*, Frankfurt am Main 1959; E. Lemberg, *Nationalismus* I/II, Reinbek bei Hamburg 1964; E. Kedourie, *Nationalism*, London 1969; H. Seton-Watson, *Nations and States*, Boulder, Co 1977; H. A. Winkler (ed.), *Nationalismus*, Königstein 1978; B. Anderson, *Imaged Communities*, London 1983; E. Gellner, *Nations and Nationalism*, Oxford 1983; I. Berlin, *Der Nationalismus*, Frankfurt 1981; P. Alter, *Nationalismus*, Frankfurt 1985; T. Mayer, *Prinzip Nation*, Opladen 1986; K. Hübner, *Das Nationale*, Graz 1991; D. Kluxen-Pyta, *Nation und Ethos*, Freiburg 1991; T. Schieder, *Nationalismus und Nationalstaat*, Göttingen ²1992.

25. Thus the conclusion of Dierse and Rath, 'Nation, Nationalismus, Nationalität', in Ritter and Gründer, *Historisches Wörterbuch* (n.8), 406–44: 411.

26. R. Koselleck, 'Volk, Nation, Nationalismus, Masse', in O. Brunner, W. Conze, R. Koselleck (eds.), *Geschichtliche Grundbegriffe* 7, Stuttgart 1992, 141ff.: 142.

27. Cf. T. Schieder, 'Idee und Gestalt des übernationalen Staates seit dem 19. Jahrhundert', in *Nationalismus und Nationalstaat* (n.24), 38ff.

28. Thus e.g. B. Geisen, introduction to *Nationale und kulturelle Identität*, Frankfurt am Main 1991, 9ff.

29. Ibid., 12, 14.

30. W. I. Thomas, *The Child in America*, New York 1928, 572. Cf. the remark by Seton Watson, *Nations and States* (n.24), 5: 'A nation exists when a significant number of people in a community act as if they were to form a nation'.

31. K. Hübner, *Das Nationale*, Graz 1991, 229 and passim.

32. Ibid., 258.

33. Cf. K. Hübner, *Die Wahrheit des Mythos*, Munich 1985, esp 349ff. ('Der mythische Begriff der Nation').

34. Ibid., 286, 290 and 281.

35. Ibid., 186, cf. Hübner, *Das Nationale* (n.31), 357ff.

36. Hübner, *Das Nationale*, 285.

37. Thus e.g. Lemberg, *Nationalismus* (n.24), who speaks of the ideology of the integration of large groups.

38. Winkler, introduction to *Der Nationalismus* (n.24), 5ff.: 34.

39. Here Christian theology should be particularly careful: precisely if they exercise influence, such myths belong to those 'powers and authorities' which are mentioned in Ephesians and Colossians; cf. H. Schlier, *Mächte und Gewalten im Neuen Testament*, Freiburg 1958.

40. I have already outlined the thesis developed here in my 'Eschatologie und Politik', in *Religion – Wissenschaft – Kultur, Jahrbuch der Wiener Katholischer Akademie* 23, 1972/3, 58ff., and in 'Christen – Nationen – Europa: Fragen und die Kirche', in *Christen – Nationen – Europa (44. Internationaler Kongress 'Kirche in Not')*, to be published 1996 by Albertus Magnus College, Königstein.

41. Emmanuel Joseph Sieyès, *Was ist der dritte Stand?* (1789, revised 1796), quoted here from the German edition, Berlin 1924, 99. For its label 'the most successful pamphlet of all time', cf. E. Schmitt, 'Sieyes', in H. Maier, H. Rausch, H. Denzer (eds.), *Klassiker des politischen Denkens* II, Munich 1968, 135ff.: 142.

42. Ibid., 94, 95.

43. Cf. Schmitt, 'Sieyes' (n.41); J. L. Talmon, *Die Ursprünge der totalitären Demokratie*, Cologne and Opladen 1961, 68.

44. J. J. Rousseau, *Le contrat social* (1761), Book III, ch. 4.

45. For this and what follows see ibid., Book II, ch. 7.

46. See I. Fetscher, *Rousseaus politische Philosophie*, Neuwied/Rheingau 1960, 72.

47. Ibid., 113.

48. Cf. Schmitt, 'Sieyes' (n.40), 150.

49. Herder thinks that every people has 'its measure of happiness' and regards the 'prejudice' as 'good, in its time, since it brings happiness. It forces peoples towards their centre', so that something positive is gained from 'limited nationalism' (according to Koselleck, 'Volk, Nation, etc.' [n.26], 317, 318); nevertheless in the course of the development he thinks a 'purified patriotism' worth striving for; this he contrasts with a 'national arrogance': every people must learn that '"no people is the only people on earth elected by God . . ." So too no people in Europe may cut itself off from others and foolishly say "All wisdom is with me"' (after H. König, *Zur Geschichte der Nationalerziehung in Deutschland*, Berlin 1960, 330f.).

50. Cf. H. de Lubac, *Corpus Mysticum*, Paris 1949; Kantorowicz, *The King's Two Bodies* (n.20), 206ff., 218ff.

51. J. L. Talmon, *Politischer Messianismus – Die romantische Phase*, Cologne and Opladen 1963.

52. D. Easton, *A Systems Analysis of Political Life,* New York 1965; W. Münch, 'Der Begriffsapparat bei David Easton', in Dieter Oberndörfer (ed.), *Systemtheorie, Systemanalyse und Entwicklungsländerforschung*, Berlin 1971, 201ff.: 219.

53. Augustine understands a people as united by the harmonious estimation of 'things' – here *res* does not mean some objectifiable state of affairs but rather 'concern' (we should think of formulae like *res publica* or *tua res agitur*); the moral and political dignity of the community is determined by the quality of this *res*, good or bad. The reality of *civitates permixtae* stands as it were between the extremes of the true peaceful society (governed by the *amor Dei*) and robber bands (shaped by the diabolically alienating *amor sui*) (cf. *City of God*, Book XIX, ch.24).

54. See e.g. W. Weidenfeld, 'Die Identität der Deutschen – Fragen, Positionen, Perspektiven', in id. (ed.), *Die Identität der Deutschen,* Munich 1983, 13ff.: 22; id., 'Europa – aber wo liegt es?', in id. (ed.), *Die Identität Europas*, Munich 1985, 13ff.: 14.

Cf. also H. Scheider, 'Europäische Identität: Historische, kulturelle und politische Dimensionen', *Integration* 1991, 4, 16off.; the following comments in part take up this article. The text of Ernst Bloch's *The Principle of Hope* (1954), Oxford 1986, begins with the questions quoted here.

55. Thus e.g. O. Bauer, *Die Nationalitätenfrage und die Sozialdemokratie*, Vienna 1924.

56. Talcott Parsons, *Political and Social Structure*, New York 1969, 292ff.

57. Cf. P. L. Berger and T. Luckmann, *The Social Construction of Reality*, Harmondsworth 1984.

58. N. Luhmann, 'Sinn als Grundbegriff der Soziologie', in J. Habermas and N. Luhmann, *Theorie der Gesellschaft oder Sozialtechnologie,* Frankfurt am Main 1971, 25ff.: 60.

59. Cf. P. R. Hofstäter, *Gruppendynamik*, new edition Reinbek bei Hamburg 1972, 108ff. The characterization of the enemy as the (existentially) wholly other takes up Carl Schmitt.

60. O. Ranum, 'Counter-Identities of Western European Nations in the Early Modern Period: Definitions and Points of Departure', in P. Boerner (ed.), *Concepts of National Identity*, Baden-Baden 1986, 63ff. Aristotle already recognized this; the identity of a commonwealth consists primarily in the identity of its constitution (*Politics*, III.3): this, the *politeia*, makes the community as it were a political subject; it is real only by virtue of the *koinonia* of the knowledge of right and wrong and the tolerable and the intolerable, but this knowledge is institutionally articulated and established – by the authorization of normative representatives.

61. Cf. N. Hartmann, *Das Problem des geistigen Seins*, Berlin ²1949, 320ff.

62. Cf. B. Holzner and R. Robertson, 'Identity and Authority: A Problem Analysis of Processes of Identification and Authorization', in R. Robertson and B. Holzner, *Identity and Authority*, Oxford 1980, 1ff., esp. 5f., 10f., 18f., 22ff.

63. Cf. E. Voegelin, *Die Neue Wissenschaft der Politik*, Munich 1959, 60ff.; M. Hauriou, *Das Problem der Institution und zwei andere Aufsätze,* ed. R. Schnur, Darmstadt 1963.

64. F. Meinecke, *Weltbürgertum und Nat ionalstaat* (1907), Munich ⁹1963, 10ff.

65. Schieder, *Nationalismus und Nationalstaat* (n.24), 65ff., 111.

66. Ibid., 69.

67. Schieder emphasizes that the three types hardly ever appeared in a pure and unmixed form; rather, there were overlaps and combinations (70ff.).

68. Cf. D. Sternberger, *Verfassungspatriotismus*, Schriften, Vol. X, Frankfurt am Main 1990.

69. Cf. H. Schneider, 'Die Europäische Union als Staatenverbund oder als "Civitas Europa"', in A. Randelzhofer, R. Scholz and D. Wilke (eds.), *Gedächtnisschrift für Eberhard Grabitz*, Munich 1995, 667ff.

A Nation of Citizens

John Coleman

Recently, fresh attention is being focussed on the reality of modern citizenship.[1] In what does it consist? Is it mainly or only a legal status of passive entitlement *rights* or does it include active citizen *responsibilities* to shape public discourse, to contribute to the building up of the commonwealth and influence social policy, beyond the mere exercise of the vote? Is citizenship uniquely an empirical membership category – resting entirely on legal incorporation by birth or naturalization by the state – or does it rely on some appeal to universal human rights? Is citizenship rooted only in a relationship to the state, as such, or does it rest, as well, in the associational networks of civil society?[2] How should we construe the bonds between citizenship and national identity?

In this short article, I want mainly to treat aspects of citizenship as it relates to nationalism. Drawing primarily on the work of Jürgen Habermas and Michael Walzer, I have constructed an argument which contends that nationalism and modern concepts of citizenship exist in a condition of both tensile conflict and mutual inter-dependence and influence. Citizenship both depends upon nationalism and yet tempers and controls it. I will explore, in what follows, the following four theses:

Thesis 1. Modern notions of democracy and citizenship presuppose the emergence of the modern nation state. Modern nationalism, in this sense, spawned and still anchors our current sense of citizenship.
Thesis 2. Paradoxically, however, modern views of citizenship, drawing upon universalistic principles, temper, indeed undercut, to some extent, extreme nationalism.
Thesis 3. In a further anomaly, citizenship as a kind of communal identity-formation depends, in part, on a viable and healthy nationalism to provide both identity and direction to the citizen-ideal.

Thesis 4. Nationalism, in its turn, is held in check by a citizenship-role rooted not only in national identity but in civil society.

Given the constraints of limited space, I will develop each thesis only very briefly. At stake in this argument is how we can simultaneously honour the particular loyalties and identity strengths of nationalism, yet temper, through a heightened sense of citizenship, nationalism's more demonic or overly parochial tendencies. While it may be attractive to some to claim, with the scriptures, that their citizenship is really only in heaven or, with Tertullian, that they are actually citizens of the whole world, in point of fact, nationalism – when compared with alternative models of the good society – continues to exert a potent influence, even in an increasingly globally inter-connected world society.

Thesis 1. Modern citizenship grows out of and still depends on the modern nation state

In an important article, the German philosopher Jürgen Habermas captures well the tensile conflict and mutual influence between citizenship and modern nationalism. In this article, Habermas is struggling with both the issue of a pan-European sense of citizenship and the increasing diminishment of the modern nation state as a sovereign unit. He notes:

> *Natio* is the Goddess of birth and origin. *Natio*, like *gens* and *populus* and unlike *civitas*, refers to peoples and tribes who were not yet organized in political associations; indeed, the Romans often used it to refer to 'savage', 'barbaric' or pagan peoples. In this classic usage, therefore, nations are communities of people of the same descent, who are integrated geographically, in the form of settlements and neigh-bourhoods, and culturally by their common language, customs and tradition, but who are not yet politically integrated in the form of state organization.[3]

The nation originally referred to a *pre-political* unity of a community with a shared historical origin and destiny. As late as the feudal and early modern period, the majority of empires and kingdoms encompassed several different nations. In the early modern period, however, kingdoms based on contiguous territorial states with a central administration began to emerge as politically powerful.

From the sixteenth century on, only such nation states could guarantee the infrastructure for rational administration and provide the legal framework for free sovereign collective and individual action. As Habermas notes, 'the modern state laid the foundations for cultural and ethnic homogeneity on the basis of which it thus proved possible to push ahead with the democratization of government since the late eighteenth century, although this was achieved at the cost of excluding ethnic minorities'.[4]

The French Revolution represents a watershed. The modern nation state and democracy have grown under the shadow of modern nationalism. As a result, since the French Revolution and through its spreading ideology into the nineteenth century, the 'nation' has changed its fundamental meaning. If before a nation designated a pre-political entity of shared common historical origin and destiny, after the eighteenth century it came to mean almost its opposite: a politically organized sovereign entity, defining in turn the political and social identity of the citizen within a democratic polity.

The manner in which national identity determines citizenship began to be reversed when people started to conceive of the nation as, fundamentally, a nation of citizens. The republican strand of citizenship, revived by Machiavelli, Montesquieu and Rousseau, saw the nation no longer as pre-political but as: (a) a self-determining political community; (b) taking concrete legal and political shape by means of an explicit constitution; and (c) as the source of state sovereignty. The intellectual seeds were sown for the twentieth-century preoccupation (post-Versailles and, again, post-1989) that each distinctive and viable nation has, indeed, its own state apparatus.

As we will note in the next thesis, paradoxically, as the nation became conflated with the concept of the nation state, the relation between citizenship and national identity strongly reversed itself. As a result, citizenship could, in principle, be uncoupled from national identity. Thus, for example, Article Four of the Revolutionary Constitution of 1793, which defined the status of the French citizen, gave to every adult foreigner who lived for one year in France not just the right to remain within the country but also all the active rights of a citizen.

Even today, democratic citizenship still continues to function exclusively within national boundaries. But because of the reversal of the relation between national citizenship and national identity (by which the nation becomes a self-organized political entity of active citizens), we can now, in principle at least, loosen the semantic connections between the two concepts. We need also to take into account that the classic form of the nation state is, at present, disintegrating. As the American sociologist,

Daniel Bell, has noted in a much quoted aphorism: the nation is too small for many of the most pressing current economic, legal and political problems and too large for many others.

Habermas can ask whether there can ever be such a thing as *European* citizenship, in the sense of 'an obligation toward the European commonwealth'.[5] As late as 1974, the French political scientist, Raymond Aron, replied to this question with a resounding No! Yet, if the semantic loosening between nationalism and citizenship (at least in the European case) can justify Habermas' inquiry about a trans-national European citizenship, it is important to recall that the genuine set of civil, political and social rights which accrue to modern citizens does not, as yet, reach beyond national borders.[6] In that sense, even today, both democracy and citizenship remain in the shadow of nationalism. As many have noted, the European community (and analogous trans-national organizations), for all of their economic and political ties, still suffer from a democratic deficit. Moreover, one can only 'belong' to the European community by first obtaining citizenship in one of its member states.

Thesis 2. Modern views of citizenship temper, even undercut, forms of extreme nationalism

Modern republican concepts of citizenship shift the traditional emphasis from *hereditary* to *acquired* nationalism. Even native-born citizens must still, in some sense, earn and validate their citizenship rights by exercising active citizenship virtues. Convicted prisoners, in default of this active exercise, can be deprived, legitimately, of certain rights of citizenship.

Democracy, in particular, transforms citizenship by transmuting the early modern idea of a self-determining political community (as mere national sovereignty, no matter the form of government) to a self-determining political community whose sovereignty derives from the people, as such, who found, guide and direct the nation state through a constitution and democratic procedures.

Ernest Renan's well known republican aphorism, 'The existence of a nation . . . is a daily plebiscite', already militates against extreme forms of hereditary nationalism. 'After 1871, Renan was only able to counter the German Empire's claims to the Alsace by referring to the inhabitants' French nationality because he could conceive of the "nation" as a nation of citizens. The nation of citizens does not derive its identity from some common ethnic and cultural properties but rather from the *praxis* of citizens who exercise their civil rights.'[7]

Thus, as Habermas argues:

> In democratic states, which understand themselves as an association of free and equal citizens, membership depends on the principle of voluntariness. Here, the usual ascriptive characteristics of domicile and birth (*jus soli* and *jus sanguinis*) by no means justify a person's being irrevocably subjected to the sovereign authority of that country. They function merely as administrative criteria for attributing to citizens an assumed, implicit concurrence, to which the legal right to emigrate or to renounce one's citizenship corresponds.[8]

To renounce one's citizenship and to emigrate are inherent political rights in modern democracies. Such a right to emigrate, among other places firmly announced in Catholic social teaching, means that one can, in fact, change national identities and allegiances. Such a right to emigration is rooted in more universal philosophical principles.[9] Indeed, in democratic polities the most fundamental modern rights of citizens to legally and constitutionally guaranteed immunities and liberties, social rights and the rights of participation always contain, at least implicitly, a universalistic core, composed of universal human rights.[10] Increasingly, it is to this universalistic core of human rights that citizen-dissident movements appeal in moves to reform or institute for the first time, in their nation state, legally guaranteed democratic citizenship rights which do not, as yet, exist. Positive legal citizen rights enshrine, in part, this larger claim to a more universal grounding in human rights.

What distinguishes modern democratic citizenship from feudal and other pre-modern views which determined people's political status by their religious, ethnic or class membership, is precisely this anchoring of citizenship rights in a more universalistic core of human rights. Hence, 'the organization of society on the basis of rights or claims that derive from group membership is sharply opposed to the concept of society based on citizenship'.[11]

The American philosopher John Rawls can even claim that the *prime* source of citizen unity in modern democratic societies is a shared conception of justice. 'Although a well-ordered society is divided and pluralistic . . . public agreement on questions of political and social justice supports ties of civic friendship and secures the bonds of association.'[12] Indeed, most modern theorists of citizenship appeal to the twin concepts of *democracy* (i.e. an agreement on fair, impartial and equal procedures to which all citizens, no matter what their religious, ethnic and linguistic status, have open access) and *justice* as the two radical sources of modern citizenship identity and the primary legitimacy for the modern nation-state.[13] In Thesis 3 we shall see that these two are not, as yet, a *sufficient* anchoring for modern citizenship.

Before turning to Thesis 3, however, we can note the ways the more universalistic citizenship rights temper, indeed to some extent undercut, extreme nationalism. Construing the nation as a nation of citizens means, for example:

1. That we must extend to ethnic or national minorities within the nation equal citizenship rights to association, free speech, political suffrage etc. Citizen-rights can not accrue only to a hegemonic ethnic group.

2. That we can not merely 'finesse' the larger questions of a right to political asylum: to immigrate to new nations; to provide legally enshrined protections and security (based on human rights) for resident non-citizen aliens living in a foreign nation, even to the point of granting partial or full citizenship rights to such resident aliens.[14]

Blood and soil can no longer be absolutized in any multi-ethnic nation state which conceives of itself as a nation of citizens and which grounds its precision of legally enshrined citizenship-rights in a more universalistic core of basic human rights. In this regard, Habermas notes, with approval, the argument put forth in the 31 October 1990 judicial decision of the Federal German Constitutional Court.

Although the court did not approve, on that occasion, the constitutionality of the right of foreigners to vote in German municipal and district elections, it did recognize clearly the legitimacy of the basic principles of the petitioners to the court who had sought such communal rights for resident foreigners: 'Behind this interpretation obviously stands the notion that it corresponds to the democratic idea, especially as it contains the idea of liberty, that there is a congruence between the possessor of democratic political rights and those subject to a specific state power. *This is the proper starting point* . . .'[15] In a profound sense, citizenship rights, in a nation of citizens, are tied to something larger than mere membership in the ethnic community and nation. They appeal to a more universal set of human rights and these rights, in part, apply even to non-citizens. Moreover, inasmuch as citizenship-rights involve an elaboration and concretion of human rights, as such, they stand above and in judgment of the action of the nation state. No nation state enjoys *absolute* and untrammelled sovereignty.

Thesis 3. Citizenship, as a kind of communal identity formation, depends, in part, on a healthy nationalism to provide both identity and direction to the citizen-ideal

A careful reading of the literature on the theory and practice of citizenship uncovers a further anomaly of mutual dependence between citizenship and nationalism. Especially, the literature devoted to the need for citizenship virtue is illuminating. Some level of civic virtue and public spiritedness seems required for modern democracies to function well.[16]

Public policy must be able to rely on responsible life-style decisions and to draw upon a reservoir of civic virtue and public spiritedness in the populace. For example:

> The state will be unable to provide adequate health care if citizens do not act responsibly with respect to their own health, in terms of a healthy diet, exercise, and the consumption of liquor and tobacco; the state will be unable to meet the needs of children, the elderly, or the disabled if citizens do not agree to share this responsibility by providing some care for their relatives; the state cannot protect the environment if citizens are unwilling to reduce, reuse, and recycle in their own homes; the ability of the government to regulate the economy can be undermined if citizens borrow immoderate amounts or demand excessive wage increases; attempts to create a fairer society will flounder if citizens are chronically intolerant of difference . . . Without cooperation and self-restraint in these areas, the ability of liberal societies to function successfully progressively diminishes.[17]

As we saw in the earlier thesis, some theorists such as John Rawls (or indeed, Habermas) seem content to appeal to justice or democracy as the all-sufficient grounding for citizenship virtues and responsibilities. That two national groups share the selfsame principles of justice, however, does not necessarily imply that we should join them together or keep them from splitting apart. Thus, the fact that Norway and Sweden share, in general, the same principles of justice, generates no strong reason for them to lament the secession of Norway from Sweden in 1905. 'A shared conception of justice throughout a political community does not necesarily generate a shared identity, let alone a shared citizenship identity that will supersede rival identities based on ethnicity.'[18]

Anglophones and Francophones in Canada, in general, share analogous principles of justice. This, on its own, need not impede moves to split Canada into two nations. The Quebequois and Anglophones can assume that their new nation states would respect the selfsame principles of justice. We need, then, a theory of citizenship which is not, reductively, only a theory of democracy or justice.

The Canadian philosopher Charles Taylor has persuasively argued that mere appeals to justice and democracy to ground citizenship remain much too 'thin'. In Taylor's view, even the model experiments in *constitutional* patriotism, such as France and the United States, have always relied on many of the trappings of nationalism and nation-states, including appeals to founding myths, national symbols and ideals of historical and quasi-ethnic or nationalist myths.[19] As the political scientist Wayne Norman puts it, 'If governments wish to use citizenship identity to promote national unity, they will have to identify citizenship, not only with the principles of justice but also with an emotional-affective sense of identity, based perhaps on a manipulation of shared symbols or historical myths.'[20]

In the end, modern notions of citizenship need to be anchored not just in universalistic principles but in a concrete narrative and myth of both origin and destiny. Citizenship loyalties, especially inasmuch as they motivate true commitments and solidarity, are not just to some abstract ideal but to a people and its unifying history. The universalistic principles of democratic states still need an anchoring in the concrete political culture of each country. The principles laid down in the constitution can neither take shape in real social practices nor become the driving force for the historical project of actually creating an association of free and equal persons unless and until they are truly *situated* in the history of the nation of citizens in such a way that concrete symbols and narratives link up to the citizens' motives, convictions and sense of communal identity as a people. If modern notions of a nation of citizens temper extreme nationalism, they remain, nonetheless, tied to the strengths and luring power of a healthy and functioning nationalism. Modern nationalism is not simply subordinate to or sycophant upon the notion of citizenship. The citizen ideal remains tied to and dependent upon, and draws its concrete motivating power from, the continued energies of nationalism in the modern period.

Thesis 4. Nationalism, in its turn, is held in check by a citizenship-role rooted not only in national identity but in civil society

If citizenship ideals remain rooted in national myths and narratives, they are anchored, as well, in loyalties to sub-national units such as the family, associations, regions, churches. Civil society theorists of citizenship, at least since Alexis de Tocqueville, emphasize that the virtues of civility and self-restraint necessary for a healthy democracy cannot be sufficiently learned either in the market or in political participation in the nation state.

These theorists look to the voluntary organizations of civil society – churches, families, labour unions, ethnic associations, cooperatives, environmental and women's support groups, neighbourhood associations, charities – as the primary schools of democratic virtue where we learn mutual obligation and trust. As the American political philosopher Michael Walzer puts it, 'the civility that makes democratic politics possible can only be learned in the associational networks of civil society'.[21]

Because membership of these groups is voluntary, failure to meet our responsibilities within them generates disapproval rather than legal sanctions. Such disapproval, however, coming as it does from family, colleagues, comrades, friends, is a more powerful lure to act responsibly than any punishment exacted by the impersonal state. In civil society, in its associational networks, human character, competence and our capacities to exercise a responsible citizenship are forged. In these smaller units (not always derivative from or congenial to the nation-state), we learn to internalize the sense of personal responsibility and mutual obligation and trust. Respect for the impersonal law of the state depends on this prior moral bonding. We learn primarily in the units of civil society that voluntary self-restraint which is essential to responsible citizenship.[22]

One of the first obligations of citizenship, then, is to participate in civil society. As Walzer puts it: 'Join the association of your choice . . . is not a slogan to rally political militants, and yet that is what civil society requires.'[23] As units independent of the state, as such, the associations of civil society which generate citizenship virtues also temper any too pretentious or totalitarian claims for the nation.

Conclusion

Conceiving of the nation as a nation of citizens reverses earlier conceptions of the relation of citizenship and national identity. While citizenship remains anchored in the nation state, it tempers extreme nationalism and demands, in the civil society linkage to citizenship, a pluralist, associational and more democratic nationalism. The modern citizenship ideal appeals beyond mere nationalism to universal human rights and below the nation state to competing loyalties to concrete associations.

Notes

1. Will Kymlicka and Wayne Norman, 'Return of the Citizen: A Survey of Recent Work on Citizen Theory', *Ethics* 104 (January 1994), 352–81.

2. Jean Cohen and Andrew Arato, *Civil Society and Political Theory*, Cambridge, Mass. 1994.

3. Jürgen Habermas, 'Citizenship and National Identity: Some Reflections on Europe', *Praxis International*, 12.1, April 1992, 3.

4. Habermas, 'Citizenship' (n.3).

5. Habermas, citing P. Kielmannsegg, 'Ohne Historisches Vorbild', in *Frankfurter Allgemeine Zeitung*, 7 December 1990.

6. T. H. Marshall distinguishes civil, political and social rights of citizens in his classic, *Citizenship and Social Class*, Cambridge 1950.

7. Habermas, 'Citizenship' (n.3), 3.

8. Ibid., 5.

9. The Catholic enunciation of a right to emigrate is found in the encyclical *Pacem in Terris*, 25. Michael Walzer makes a philosophical case for this right in his *Spheres of Justice*, New York 1983, 39–40.

10. See Judith Shklar, *American Citizenship*, Cambridge, Mass. 1991.

11. John Porter, *The Measure of Canadian Society*, Ottawa 1987, 128.

12. John Rawls, 'Kantian Construction in Moral Theory', *Journal of Philosophy* 77, 1980, 540.

13. See Geoff Andrews, *Citizenship*, London 1991.

14. Walzer, *Spheres of Justice* (n.9), 56–61.

15. Cited in Habermas, 'Citizenship' (n.3), 14.

16. For citizenship virtue theory see Stephen Macedo, *Liberal Virtues: Citizenship, Virtue and Community*, Oxford 1990.

17. Kymlicka and Norman, 'Return of the Citizen' (n.1), 360.

18. Ibid., 376.

19. Charles Taylor, *Multiculturalism and the Politics of Recognition*, Princeton 1992.

20. Kymlicka and Norman, 'Return of the Citizen' (n.1), 377.

21. Michael Walzer, 'The Civil Society Argument', in Chantel Mouffe, *Dimensions of Radical Democracy*, London 1992, 104.

22. See Mary Ann Glendon, *Rights Talk*, New York 1991, 109.

23. Walzer, 'The Civil Society Argument' (n.21), 106.

III · The Role of Religion in National Conflicts

Religion and Churches and the Post-Yugoslav War

Srdjan Vrcan

1. There are four preliminary points to underline.

First, the war in former Yugoslavia has not been accidental, fallen from the clouds nobody knows why and how. On the contrary, it has been an easily predictable war, caused almost necessarily by political strategies, becoming dominant in the mid-1980s, the fundamental feature of which has been that they have been moving since the beginning of the Yugoslav crisis along collision courses. In this sense, the war has confirmed von Klausewitz' thesis that war is but the continuation of politics by other means.

Second, the fundamental feature of the political strategies, having led to the war, has been that they have been pursuing (with the initial exception of the Bosnian Muslims) Mazzini's formula 'One nation, one state. Only one state for every nation', in diametrically opposed terms.

Third, it is mostly believers and those of different religions who have been mutually facing one another with arms in their hands.

Fourth, the political strategies, having led to political violence and ultimately to arms, have been legitimized by respective religious organizations (primarily the Croatian Catholic Church and the Serbian Orthodox Church).[1]

This is the challenge to be faced, basically taking into account the nature of legitimacy in religious terms.

2. There is no doubt that the dominant political strategies ought to be described as nationalist. Consequently, the crux of the challenge is the relation of religion and churches to nationalism(s).

It is possible to elude this problem by differentiating between patriotism and nationalism, and linking the legitimacy to patriotism and not nationalism. It is possible to do the same by distinguishing between benign and un-benign, non-arrogant and arrogant, defensive and aggressive nationalism, etc., which is being done in particular when justifying the legitimacy in terms of the doctrine of a just war. However, this has been done equally by all three major religions involved.

It seems more plausible to start by defining nationalism as has been done by some contemporary sociologists and historians (e.g. Ernest Gellner, Anthony Smith, John Breuilly, Lisbet Hoogh, Eric Hobsbawm, etc.).

First, nationalism claims that the social category it represents is culturally distinct, and it demands explicit recognition of its distinctiveness, but it demands primarily the reorganization of the state structure so that the organization of the political realm expresses ethnic distinctiveness.[2] Basically, 'nationalism is a theory of political legitimacy, which requires that ethnic boundaries should not cut across political ones, and, in particular, that ethnic boundaries within a given state – a contingency already excluded by the principle in its general formulation – should not separate the power-holders from the rest'.[3] This is the essence of the nationalist imperative in Ernest Gellner's terms.

Second, nationalism rejects violations of or deviations from the nationalist imperative. The mono-national state is considered to be the normal and ideal state.

Third, the notion of nationhood is considered to be above all other political notions, and national interests with loyalty to the nation are conceived of as coming before and standing above other possible interests and loyalties.[4]

Fourth, national culture is envisioned as an homogenous entity to be distinguished from other cultures, and to be protected in the clash of mutually irreconcilable cultures by the respective national states. This is the essence of the formula 'One culture, one nation, one state'. F. Ferrarotti has described this notion of culture as follows: 'Different cultures are conceived of as realities closed in themselves and self-sufficient, supplied by a high degree of coherence so that they do not support any kind of "loans" from outside, as genuine "no shopping wholes" (*sic*), therefore as crystallized realities mutually absolutely incommunicable, irreconcilable, least of all able to integrate.'[5] Consequently, a multicultural society is depicted as a counternatural construct, inevitably generating conflicts and racism.[6]

Fifth, national identity is perceived as exclusive, immutable, non-negotiable, pre-given. Consequently, the notion of identity as a dynamic reality which gives and accepts contributions of other identities and is changing, being redefined and reformulated through time and in a communication with other cultures and other socio-economic and historic-institutional aspects,[7] is rejected.

Finally, nationalism includes a vision of the world. Mankind is 'really' and 'naturally' divided into distinct communities, analogous to the divisions of species in the animal world. This point has been controversial. Anthony Smith insists that nationalism operates with the vision of mankind as composed essentially by equal and free nations, each giving a particular contribution of its own to the development of the world.[8] Therefore he contests the thesis that, because of their racism, Italian Fascism and German Nazism were nationalisms in their extreme forms. The opposite point of view is that usually nationalism includes at least *in nuce* an asymmetrical or hierarchical vision of cultures and, therefore, a hierarchical view of the family of nations. Eric Hobsbawm maintains that there is no world of free and equal nations, but only a world in which some potential national groups, claiming that status, impede other analogous groups in making the same claims.[9] Ernest Gellner notes that 'not all nationalism can be satisfied at any rate at the same time' so that 'the satisfaction of some spells the frustration of others'.[10]

This applies to all kinds of nationalisms, and it certainly covers current nationalisms in former Yugoslavia.

3. Some clarifications ought to be made.

First, nationalism is a contradictory phenomenon which Anthony Giddens compares with the two-faced Greek god Janus,[11] with one or the other face becoming more prominent in different historical situations. It means that there are not two clearly distinct types of nationalism with an unsurmountable abyss between them, but only a mixture of contradictory features with their historically changing balance. Consequently, there is a possibility of a shift from nationalism to chauvinism, from a moderate one to an aggressive one, from benign to un-benign etc.

The contradictory nature of nationalism has become very visible in the events in former Yugoslavia.

One must certainly admit that dominant political strategies, pursuing the nationalist imperative of the necessary congruence between the state and nation, have had an initial democratic potential. There is no doubt that the claim to the self-government of a nation has a democratic legitimacy. This has been underlined by Jürgen Habermas: 'The nation state and democracy were born as twin brothers from the French

Revolution."[12] Therefore, sometimes links between human rights and democracy with nationalism are described as irrefutable.

However, the right to national self-government has been applied by nationalisms in a very selective way, i.e. by turning it practically into a kind of chameleon right,[13] that is, a right which is unconditionally crucial for one's own nation, but is not crucial in the same way for some other nation. There is nothing astonishing in the fact that the right to self-government, applied in such a way, results in the best case in discrimination of some minorities, and in the introduction of a crucial distinction between first-order citizens who are included in the state in a *pactum unionis* and second-order citizens or subjects, to be included in the same state on the basis of a *pactum subjectionis*, in Hobbes' terms, and in the worst case in armed conflicts, exclusions and genocide.

Secondly, it is the nationalist imperative to induce violence. It is ultimately the congruence between boundaries that must be frequently imposed and enforced. Bosnia and Herzegovina are only the tragic example in that respect. Therefore it is no wonder that conformity to the nationalist imperative has been bound 'to involve population exchanges or expulsions, more or less forcible assimilation, and sometimes liquidation, in order to attain that close relation between the state and culture which is the essence of nationalism'.[14] It may be argued, therefore, that the course of events in former Yugoslavia has so far fully confirmed Ernest Gellner's thesis of the essence of the nationalist imperative and Eric Hobsbawm's conclusion that the territorial homogenous national state is a political programme which can be usually realized only by barbarians and by barbaric means.[15]

Furthermore, it has been suggested that the identification of the state with a culture and the ensuing politicization of culture may be inaugurating extreme social conflicts and even a new war – hot or cold[16] – since it requires that specific cultural values are to be recognized as authoritative by all in a society, i.e. taking culture as the absolute normative entity, contiguous with the political order. Alain Touraine has indicated some consequences of such a politicization of culture, warning that when conflicts become conflicts between cultures, there is no possible mediation, no possible community of beliefs and practices, and social conflicts are replaced by affirmations of absolute differences and the total rejections of the others.

The politicization of culture at the same time has an evident authoritarian charge. This has been indicated by Touraine, who defines democracy in a way which is hardly compatible with the formula of 'one culture, one state'. 'When the state is defined as the expression of a collective, political, social and cultural being – the nation, the people – or, what is more grave, of a God or a principle of which this people, this nation and itself have been the privileged agents and which they are called to defend, democracy is not in operation any more, even if the economic framework allows certain public liberties to persist. Democracy is based upon the free creation of a political order, upon the sovereignity of the people, and therefore upon freedom of choice in respect of all cultural heritage.'[17] Consequently, conflicts are generated and legitimatized by the formula 'one nation, one state', as well as by the wider formula 'one culture, one nation and one state', applied to a multi-cultural and multi-national area. Alain Touraine has indicated the political consequences of different notions of the nation state. 'Democratization transforms a community into a society regulated by law and the state representing the society itself, at the same time as a power limited by the fundamental laws. The opposite notion which may be called popular, *völkisch*, remembering that this has been the term the Nazis used to describe their regime, imposes a fundamental unity, beyond any possible choice, which establishes a nationalism incompatible in principle with democracy.'[18]

4. The role of religions and churches in the post-Yugoslav war may be analysed from two different angles: in respect of the role of religions and churches in the exacerbation of social divisions and cleavages along national lines in the grave social crisis, and in respect of the role of religions and churches in the war in post-Yugoslavia.

It seems that the traditionally dominant religions and churches have played an important part in exacerbating social divisions and social cleavages in two crucial ways. First, they have contributed to the exacerbation of these divisions by facilitating their projection to an overarching quasi-ontological or grand-historical background and presenting them as divisions and cleavages between essentially irreconcilable human types, basically counterposed types of cultures and incommunicable types of civilizations. Consequently, they have contributed towards extracting current political conflicts from their concrete contemporary social and political environment, and presenting them as centuries-long conflicts between essentially opposed human types, types of cultures and civilizations. Secondly, they have contributed to creating a visible Manichaean dualism of the partners in conflicts, presenting the one side as quasi-immaculate and as the side of the Good as such, and depicting the other in demoniacal or satanic terms as the incarnation of Evil as such. In this way, they have contributed towards turning the existing political conflicts into conflicts of cultures with consequences described by A. Touraine.

5. It is interesting to raise the question why such legitimacy has been given. One may recall Weber's thesis that there is a permanent tension between religion operating with the idea of universal human brotherhood and politics which is always involved with power and violence.[19] Furthermore, it may be mentioned that the rise of nationalism has been frequently linked to secularization and even described as the religion of modernization. However, we should not forget, that, as Freeman recently stressed, 'nationalism is not only like religion in the way it grounds its political values, but it is often combined with religion as a source of justification. While some religious commitments are sub-national or trans-national, they can easily be mobilized for nationalist purposes.'[20]

The first answer is connected to the fall of the Communist regime. In substance, the nationalist political strategies have evidently been interpreted as the most efficient shock therapy, to be supported in order to eliminate all traces of the former Communist regime and ideology. Religion is the most promising alternative to atheistic Communism in terms of radical change in the systemic position of religion and the respective church. At the same time, the religions have been welcome as the best and most rapid way to democracy.

The second answer takes into consideration some traditional components in the religious culture of the respective operative religions.

(a) There is no doubt that the traditional religious cultures of Croatian Catholicism, Serbian Orthodoxy and Bosnian Islam have included the idea of a fusion between the respective religion and the nation. Therefore religion is described as the essential constituent of the national being and the very essence of the respective nationhood as well as the ultimate bulwark of that nationhood. In such circumstances the politicization of culture basically becomes the politicization of religion, and it is the religion which becomes central in distinctions between 'we' and 'them'.

(b) Furthermore, there is an identification between what is described as the religious cause (Catholic, Orthodox and/or Islamic) and a national cause (Croatian, Serbian and/or Bosnian Muslim). Consequently, to engage in the promotion and defence of a religious cause is traditionally interpreted to mean engaging in the promotion and defence of the respective national cause, and vice versa.

(c) There is a belief in a synthesis between religion and national state. It is the national state which is considered to offer the best and necessary political cover for the promotion of religious culture and church activity. Therefore, to stand with the respective nation as such has also meant standing with the respective national state and its politics.

(d) There is a peculiar view of national history which persists in dominant religious cultures. The main feature of this view is that national history in each case has been described as a long-term tragedy. Consequently, the Serbian national history has been described as a martyrology of the Serbian people; the Croatian national history as a Calvary of the Croatian nation; the history of Bosnian Islam as a past and present holocaust of Muslim populations. Furthermore, such a national history has been interpreted as a consequence of the exceptional dedication of the respective nation through centuries to celestial values and to God. Therefore, it is believed that there is a privileged place for the respective nation in the plans of providence, as well as a privileged relationship for centuries between it and God.

(e) There is a view of the specific position of the religion and church in the region which still survives. This position is described in terms of a religion and church being for centuries on the frontier, permanently exposed to attacks and pressures from outside. In the case of Croatian Catholicism this is described by the term *antemurale Christianitatis*; in the case of Serbian Orthodoxy by the term Orthodoxy on the frontier, exposed for centuries to the pressure of Roman Catholicism as well as of Islamic penetration; in case of Bosnian Islam as the promontory of the Islamic world and Islamic culture on European soil.

(f) Traditions still survive which refer to religious others in the region as enemies, historically described as schismatic or as infidel. These are reactivated and recycled when needed. The most recent case, for instance, has occurred during the armed conflicts between Croatians and Muslims in Central Bosnia and Herzegovina.

Consequently, there is a traditional belief in 'a special people, a sacred land, national purity, a heroic task, a utopian future and war against enemies of the ideal' in the operative religious cultures, which can easily be activated on behalf of nationalist political strategies.

So it is not astonishing that the traditionally dominant religions could have served as the basis of legitimacy (with the initial exception of the Bosnian Islams) for the political strategies, which basically prove Mazzini's formula 'One nation, one state. Only one state for every nation.' This legitimacy, of course, has been of a quite specific nature: it has been political legitimacy in superior and almost numinous terms.

6. There have been shifts in the attitudes of religions and churches in the course of the crisis. It may be assumed that such shifts have been motivated by the experience of flagrant violations of human rights caused by nationalist strategies, and by brutality and crimes committed on a mass scale in a dirty war. However, such assumptions cannot be plausibly substantiated. In practice no church has confirmed itself by its public and unequivocal acts as the first and most coherent defender of the universality of human rights at the level of everyday life for all persons actually persecuted or threatened, regardless of their nationality, faith, political orientations, etc. At the same time, the churches' attitudes to brutality and war crimes have been very ambiguous, consisting (*a*) in very abstract condemnations of brutality and war crimes in general; (*b*) in very abstract invitations to their flocks to abstain from such acts; (*c*) in very strong and explicit condemnations of brutalities and war crimes committed by the other side; (*d*) in silence over the brutality and war crimes of their own side; and (*e*) an almost total lack of public protection of the victims of war brutalities experienced by others.

Such shifts have been motivated basically by other reasons. They may be described as a change from unconditional and total legitimacy given previously to the dominant political strategies to some kind of conditional and limited legitimacy, as well as an erosion of the previous religious unanimity in this respect. This is most evident in the Serbian Orthodox Church in the latest dissent with the official Serbian state politics, particularly in regard to Bosnia. However, a kind of retraction of previously given legitimacy has been endorsed by the same nationalist political strategy and its proclaimed aims.

The shift in Croatian Catholicism has been not on the strategic level of the current official Croatian state politics, but on some tactical levels, primarily regarding the state politics on Bosnia and Herzegovina and, secondly, very recently, referring partially to protection of human rights in Croatia as well as in some theologians' growing distancing from nationalism. The shift in Bosnian Islam is to be interpreted in terms of the increasing rigidity of the Islamic dimensions of the Bosnian state.

Notes

1. It is not that 'resurgent nationalist ideologies have been looking for support in religious doctrines as today in former Yugoslavia' (Mgr. König, 'Pourquoi il faut dialoguer avec les autres religions', *Le Monde* 18–19 June 1994, B–9); rather, there has been a reciprocal quest for mutual support.

2. Lisbet Hoogh, 'Nationalist Movements and Social Factors. Theoretical Perspective', in J. Okaley (ed.), *The Social Origin of Nationalist Movements*, London 1992, 21.

3. Ernest Gellner, *Nation and Nationalism*, Oxford 1986, 1.

4. John Breuilly, *Nationalism and the State*, Manchester 1982, 3.

5. Franco Ferrarotti, *La tentazione dell'oblio*, Rome and Bari 1993, 187.

6. Tomislav Sunić, 'The Fallacy of the Multiethnic State. The Case of Yugoslavia', *Conservative Review* 1.3, 1990, 11.

7. Franco Ferraroti's description, *La tentazione dell'oblio* (n.5), 136.

8. Anthony D. S. Smith, *Nationalism in the Twentieth Century*, Oxford 1979, 2.

9. Eric Hobsbawn, *Nation and Nationalism since 1980: Programme, Myth, Reality*, Oxford 1987.

10. Gellner, *Nation and Nationalism* (n.3), 2.

11. Anthony Giddens, *The Nation-State and Violence*, Cambridge 1992, 218.

12. Jürgen Habermas, *Faktizität und Geltung*, Frankfurt 1992, 634.

13. Benyamin Neuberger, 'Samoodločba narodov-konceptualne dileme', *Nova revija*, 141–142, 1994, 157.

14. Gellner, *Nation and Nationalism* (n.3), 101.

15. Hobsbawm, *Nation and Nationalism* (n.9).

16. Majid Tehranian, 'World With/Out Wars: Moral Spaces and the Ethics of Transnational Communication', *Javnost. The Public*, 1994. 1–2, 76.

17. Alain Touraine, *Qu'est-ce que la democratie?*, Paris 1994, 99.

18. Ibid., 100.

19. H. H. Gerth and C. W. Mills, *From Max Weber: Essays in Sociology*, New York 1958, 33–5.

20. Michael Freeman, 'Religion, Nationalism and Genocide: Ancient Judaism Revisited', *Archives Européennes de Sociologie*, 35.2, 1994, 278.

Religion, Nationalism and the Break-Up of Canada

David Seljak

The government of the province of Quebec, now led by the Parti Québécois (PQ), has promised to hold a referendum on sovereignty in the fall of 1995. The programme of the PQ has been supported by the Bloc Québécois, a separate independentist party which sits as the official opposition in Canada's federal House of Commons.[1] Sovereignty is the latest strategy pursued by French Quebeckers, who make up eighty-two per cent of the population.[2] Polls indicate that public support for sovereignty is at forty to forty-five per cent, which means that even French Quebeckers are not united on the PQ's strategy. Yet the mood in Quebec is uncertain. Even if the referendum fails as an earlier one did in 1980, the problem of coming to a consensus around the structure and meaning of Canada will continue as long as the French-speaking majority of Quebec define themselves as a nation and the majority of Canadians define French Canadians as an ethnic minority and Quebec as one province among ten with no special status.[3]

While the national question is focussed on socio-economic and cultural issues, the Catholic Church has maintained a public presence in the debate. Eighty-six per cent of all Quebeckers (total population 6,810,300) still identify themselves as Catholics. Among French Quebeckers, ninety-five per cent identify themselves as Catholics. The publicly funded school system is organized along confessional lines. The church maintains a pastoral presence in the Catholic school system (by far the larger system, representing 185 of 217 school commissions) and controls the content of religious education. Ninety-two per cent of parents of primary school children choose Catholic education over the non-confessional moral education.[4] There is some irony in this, since only twenty-nine per cent of

Quebec Catholics attend mass on Sunday (as opposed to thirty-eight per cent for Canadian Catholics outside the province).[5] While non-practising themselves, Quebec Catholics wish to see their children receive Catholic religious education. Catholicism still plays an important part of French Quebeckers' cultural identity and solidarity.

Catholicism and French Canadian identity

This close identification between Catholicism and national identity has its roots in the historical relationship of the church and the French population of the area. Before 1960, French Canadian nationalism was very closely identified with Catholicism, and the church played an important role in Quebec society. Besides controlling education, health care and social services for French Quebeckers, it also exercised a fair degree of political power and social influence through a network of Catholic Action groups, Catholic labour unions, credit unions, cooperatives, and newspapers. From 1840 to 1940, it was the Catholic Church more than the state that provided the societal framework for French Quebeckers. It must be stated that the main reason for this close identification of Catholicism and nationalism was the domination of Quebec society by a foreign political and economic elite. Several studies have shown that French Canadians were systematically disadvantaged in economic and social relations with English Canadians and Americans.[6] Two important consequences of this fact have been that French Canadians have never made up more than five per cent of the class of owners of large-scale capital and that English Canadians have occupied the most important positions in the Quebec economy.

The Catholic Church provided the economically disadvantaged and politically marginalized French Canadians with a culture of resistance and a social framework of self-expression. While the church succeeded in instilling in French Canadians a sense of pride in being different and a strategy for resisting assimilation, there were problematic aspects in traditional religious nationalism. French Canadian nationalism was frequently intolerant of religious and ethnic pluralism within Quebec society, of political or religious dissent, and of movements to democratize society or the Church. Both Quebec society and the church were marked by a high degree of clericalism. Finally, French Canadian religious nationalism was often orientated on parish rural life. This prevented French Quebeckers from adapting to urban, industrial life in a way that would allow them to compete with English-speaking Canadians.

The Quebec experience was not unique. The British sociologist David Martin has noted that often ethnic identity and Catholicism have been fused together when a population is oppressed by a foreign power. In such cases as Poland and Ireland, the identification between religion and nationalism has often been complete. In the cases of Quebec, Croatia, Slovakia, Brittany, the Basque country, and other such national enclaves within wider federations, national identity was similarly mediated by Catholicism but not in an absolute fashion. In these cases, one saw a confusion between religion and politics, a fusion of ethnic and religious identity, a high degree of clericalism, low tolerance of dissent and pluralism, and extraordinarily high levels of practice and Sunday observance.[7]

The secularization of Quebec

The situation in Quebec changed drastically after 1960. Under the Liberal Party, the state took over the church's responsibilities in education, health care and social services. French Quebeckers now looked to their state to protect the French language and culture, to increase their control over the economy, and to promote the participation of French-speakers in the upper echelons of the economy. The Quiet Revolution was both the product and promoter of a new, optimistic and dynamic nationalism in Quebec. Despite differences in ideological outlook and strategy, a consensus formed around the basic assertions of the new nationalism. Quebeckers agreed that their society should become a modern, pluralist, industrial society which should operate in French. Some of these nationalists were happy to work within the framework of confederation. These identified with the Liberal party, whose policy of national development was guided by Keynesian liberalism. Others sought to create an independent Quebec. These identified with the Parti Québécois, which adopted a social democratic position on the state's involvement in national liberation. In 1976, the PQ was elected with a majority of seats to the provincial legislature.

The politicization of French Canadian nationalism meant its secularization. Besides its loss of direct power and influence, the church had to respond to its loss of control over the central defining stories and symbols of French Canadian nationalism. As Gregory Baum has argued, the church in Quebec accepted its loss of power with relative serenity. The tragic cultural schism which marked the secularization of the French and Italian societies did not repeat itself in Quebec. Because the secularization of Quebec coincided with the Second Vatican Council, many Catholics could be critical of the old religious nationalism and the pre-conciliar church without leaving the church. Many Catholics supported the laicization of the large public bureaucracies which oversaw education, health care, welfare services. For its part, the reforming liberal elite saw the church as foundational to Quebec society. Consequently there was little political anti-clericalism. Both sides sought compromise and co-operation.[8]

Because the church did not reject the new society, Catholics were closely involved in the new nationalist political movements in the 1960s and 1970s. A minority even formed Catholic 'separatist' movements and parties. The more progressive of these groups developed into an important faction within the modern independentist movement. Even the conservative Catholic nationalist groups, the *Sociétés Saint-Jean-Baptiste*, came to support the interventionist state as crucial to the defence and development of Quebec society. Catholics involved in these groups transformed them into secular nationalist movements. But even those politically and socially active groups which wished to retain their Catholic identity came to agree with the basic assertions of the new nationalism. Only a small handful of French Catholic intellectuals, business leaders and politicians supported the constitutional *status quo* defended by the federal government.

Beyond this acceptance of the new nationalism, there was a remarkable consensus on how the church should present its opinions on the national question. The Second Vatican Council had decisively changed the relationship of the church to society. The council documents on the constitution of the church and on religious liberty clearly show that the church no longer imagined that it could control the state or hope to reconquer political society through Catholic associations or political parties. The new teaching on the relationship of the church to the 'world' allowed the Quebec hierarchy to accept the secularization of society. Meanwhile the papal social teaching, renewed in *Pacem in Terris*, inspired the church to remain a public presence, interested in the social and political problems of society. The council turned away from the dream of religious establishment but did not accept the 'privatization' of the faith. In Quebec, this meant that the church would no longer seek to embody the nation, nor would it withdraw to the task of the pastoral care of individual souls.[9]

The church and the 1980 referendum

This remarkable consensus can be seen in the participation of Catholics in the 1980 referendum on sovereignty called by the social democratic Parti Québécois. Because Quebeckers were deeply divided on the referendum question, prominent Catholics joined the committees for both the yes and no options. The church leadership permitted Catholics to voice their own opinions but insisted that the church itself not be identified with any political party or framework. The bishops, along with theologians, activists and intellectuals, sought to introduce a teaching which could provide ethical guidance while respecting the autonomy of political society and the rights of conscience of Catholics. The content and style of this ethical teaching evolved out of the Quebec church's experience of the churches which marked international Catholicism in this period. I have organized the church's teaching into the following three dominant themes.

The right to self-determination

One of the central problems in the Canada–Quebec crisis has been the definition of French Canadians. Were they a people or nation with the rights to self-determination outlined in the United Nations International Covenant on Civil and Political Rights (1966),[10] or simply an ethnic minority in the Canadian nation state? The federal government had consistently adopted the latter position. By contrast, the Canadian Catholic bishops had recognized French Canadians as a 'people' in their letter celebrating the centennial year of Confederation (1967).[11] For Catholics this was an important question, since important ecclesial documents from Paul VI's *Populorum progressio* to the World Synod of Bishops' *Justice in the World* affirmed the rights of peoples to development, justice and self-determination. In 1972, the Canadian bishops were asked by Quebec Catholics if the church's affirmation of the right to self-determination applied to the people of Quebec. In their letter, 'On Pastoral Implications of Political Choices', the episcopal conference replied that Quebeckers were free to choose any political framework that was respectful of the human person and the human community.[12] In their letter on the eve of the 1980 referendum, the bishops of Quebec were more emphatic about the right of Quebeckers to choose their collective destiny. The bishops argued that all Quebeckers, the Francophone majority, the Anglophone community, the ethnic minorities and the aboriginal peoples, shared in the right to decide the future of the 'people of Quebec'. The right to self-determination was not absolute, but carried with it certain responsibilities and duties which will be discussed below.

The legitimacy of the democratic process

Catholic groups were excited by the very process of the national debate and referendum. In the face of modern individualism and consumerism, the national debate forced people to think about the common good and social justice. It forced them to outline the values and assumptions of their *'projet de société'*. Church groups and the episcopacy welcomed the referendum debate as an important moment in the democratic development of Quebec. The debate over the type of society Quebec would become promoted 'conscientization' and participation. In August 1979, the Quebec assembly of bishops defended the democratic process in a pastoral letter printed in all the major daily newspapers.[13] They argued that individuals had a duty to take part in the debate, to refrain from demonizing their opponents, to remain open to reconciliation, and to safeguard the Christian value of respect for the dignity of the human person and community. Given the history of Quebec and the often anti-democratic positions adopted by the hierarchy, the bishops were careful to announce their neutrality on the referendum question. The gospel message, they argued, could not be directly identified with either option.

The referendum and social justice

During the 1970s, the Catholic leadership became increasingly critical of the Quebec state and society for their indifference to the suffering of the weakest citizens. Guided by the social teaching of the international church and the experience of local activists, the hierarchy released pastoral letters addressing the plight of working people, the unemployed, youths, aboriginal peoples, people living in impoverished regions, visible minorities, immigrants and refugees. This new perspective had important implications for the church's response to the new nationalism. Many Catholics recast the national question in the light of their commitment to social justice. The bishops of Quebec adopted this position in their second letter before the 1980 referendum, *'Construire ensemble une société meilleure'*. They argued that whichever side won, Quebeckers still had to work to build a society that would be more open and just. Guiding their vision of a just society there were five major themes: 1. the duty of citizens to participate in the defnition of their society; 2. the appropriate judgment of rights and duties of persons in light of the common good; 3. an equitable distribution of goods and responsibilities; 4. a serious attitude towards the spiritual and cultural elements of society; and 5. solidarity among peoples.[14] Nationalism could not be defined in a self-serving way, but had to be open to solidarity with the weakest members of society and with the world's poorest nations.

Conclusion: the Quebec church's unique contribution

While Catholic social teaching has addressed a wide variety of social and political questions, it has not dealt with the question of nationalism in a sustained manner. Anyone interested in writing a history of the church's teaching on the right of collectivities to self-determination, development and social justice, would have to patch together statements from various national churches, papal messages and ecclesial documents.[15] Given the close identification of religion and nationalism in the modern world, this lapse is curious. Given the excesses to which religious nationalism is prone, it is also dangerous.

Because Quebec's rapid secularization and nationalist re-awakening coincided with the Second Vatican Council and the emergence of the faith and justice movement within the church, the church in Quebec has developed a sustained and coherent discussion on the ethical implications of nationalism. It has taught that the right to national self-determination is an important one, but that it also carries with it certain duties, including commitment to a more open and just society, respect for ethnic and religious minorities, special attention to aboriginal peoples, openness to international society, and solidarity with the poorest nations. The exercise of the collective right to self-determination is not absolute, but has to be judged in each case. Especially important is the social project which every nationalism inherently carries with it. Does the project of a nationalist movement move society towards a more participatory and just democracy? Is it respectful of the human person and human community?

The manner in which the Quebec church put forward its message was as important as the message itself. The church has sought to engage in a public ethical debate in a way that has avoided the extremes of past participation in politics by Catholics. The church in Quebec no longer hopes to control the state nor to re-colonize political society through the organization of the laity. Instead, the church has sought to protect the integrity of Quebec's democratic political culture and to make it more open to wider participation.

This position, established in the 1960s and 1970s, has remained the consensus of the church in the present crisis. However, given the present context, the church has changed the emphasis of its response. Since 1980, both the PQ and the Liberals have adopted a 'free-market' neo-liberalism that has altered the nature of the national debate. The nationalist options, be they federalist or sovereigntist, are no longer defended in socio-cultural or ethical terms but in economic terms. Each party argues that its option will mean that Quebeckers will become more competitive in the global economy. In recent pastoral letters, publications and presentations to government-sponsored commissions on the national question, Catholic groups and the hierarchy have been consistent in insisting that national-ism cannot be justified solely in terms of getting the best deal for Quebeckers. The national debate, they have argued, must still be concer-ned with a *projet de société*, a social vision of a more just, open and solidary Quebec.

Notes

1. The Bloc Québécois had 54 MPs elected to parliament in 1993, winning in every constituency where French-speakers were a majority. The BQ recently lost a seat to the Liberal Party of Canada in a by-election.

2. All census information in this essay is taken from the 1991 Census of Canada. See Statistics Canada, *Religions in Canada*, Ottawa 1993, 240: table 7.

3. The 1980 referendum failed by a margin of 40% in favour to 60% opposed. In 1982, the federal government under Prime Minister Pierre Trudeau negotiated a deal with the nine other provincial premiers to 'repatriate' the constitution, the British North America Act (1867). The Quebec government, still led by the independentist PQ, refused to sign the new constitution. Even the officially federalist Liberal Party of Quebec refused to sign the document when they came into power in 1985. Two attempts at negotiation between the federal government and the Liberals to resolve the ongoing crisis failed, leading to the present referendum. A useful guide to the present crisis is Kenneth McRoberts, *Quebec: Social Change and Political Crisis*, Toronto 1988 (third edition; earlier editions by Kenneth McRoberts and Dale Postgate).

4. Micheline Milot, 'Le catholicisme au creuset de la culture', *Studies in Religion*, 20.1, 1991, 53.

5. Reginald Bibby, *Unknown Gods: The Ongoing Story of Religion in Canada*, Toronto 1993, 6: table 1.1. The drop in church attendance in Quebec has been astounding. In 1957, 88% of Catholic Quebeckers attended mass each Sunday.

6. The most important study was the third volume of the *Report of the Royal Commission on Bilingualism and Biculturalism* published by the federal government in the late 1960s. Relying on census data, it showed that French Canadians were at a greater occupational disadvantage in 1961 than they were in 1941.

7. David Martin, *A General Theory of Secularization*, New York 1978, 77–80.

8. Relying on the framework provided by Martin, Baum argues that this parallels the experience of the Catholic Church in Belgium. See Gregory Baum, *The Church in Quebec*, Ottawa 1991, 15–47.

9. The new identity of the church was expressed and consolidated in the report of the *Commission d'étude sur les laïcs et l'Église*, entitled *L'Église du Québec: un héritage, un projet*, Montréal 1971.

10. See especially Article 1.

11. See Canadian Catholic Conference, 'On the Occasion of the Hundredth Year of Confederation', in *Do Justice! The Social Teaching of the Canadian Catholic Bishops, 1945–1986*, ed. E. F. Sheridan SJ, Toronto 1987, 122–34. Kenneth Westhues has argued that, in its structures and policies, the Canadian Catholic Church has always condoned and promoted the 'bi-national' definition of Canada over the federalist model. See his 'Nationalisme et catholicisme canadien', *Concilium* 131, 1978, 61–8.

12. Canadian Catholic Conference, 'On Pastoral Implications of Political Choices', in *Do Justice! The Social Teaching of the Canadian Catholic Bishops, 1945–1986* (n.11), 230–2.

13. Assemblée des évêques du Québec, 'Le peuple québécois et son avenir politique: message de l'Assemblée des évêques du Québec, sur l'évolution de la société québécoise, le 15 août 1979', in *La Justice sociale comme bonne nouvelle: messages sociaux, économiques et politiques des évêques du Québec 1972–1983*, ed. Gérard Rochais, Montréal 1984, 137–44.

14. Assemblée des évêques du Québec, 'Construire ensemble une société meilleure: deuxième message de l'Assemblée des évêques du Québec sur l'évolution politique de la société québécoise, le 9 janvier 1980', in *La Justice sociale comme bonne nouvelle* (n.13), 145–56.

15. Some examples of this attempt are John J. Wright, *National Patriotism in Papal Teaching*, Boston 1942; Richard Arès, SJ, *L'Église et les projets d'avenir du peuple canadien-français*, Montréal 1974; and Pierre Charritton, *Le Droit des peuples à leur identité: l'évolution d'une question dans l'histoire du christianisme*, Montréal 1979. Cf. also J.-T. Delos, *La Nation. Tome 1 et 2*, Montréal 1944.

De profundis – Religion as the Support of Minorities

László Aszódi and Frater Georgius[1]

Nationalism, patriotism, cultural self-understanding, social identity are scholarly terms. They also have an everyday life. They can be means of humanity and also of inhumanity, and even both at the same time. They can be a Christian duty and also a crime, a tormenting dilemma. We shall attempt to reflect on our own experience, in Siebenbürgen in Roumania. Nevertheless, we do not think that we are an exception. What is worth mentioning is not our deep problems but the pressures of the minority situation. This is a challenge to individuals and society, to Christians and their churches.

We cannot stand apart from the efforts which our parents, brothers and sisters, and already their children are making to preserve their identity. But involvement threatens to become confrontation with others. As members of a minority we can complain when the majority wants an undivided nation and leaves no room for existing nationalities. We cannot change this. The sharp conflict of interest is there as a fact. And our origin and our tasks bind us to the minority, to a minority which suffers because of its language, its origin, its otherness. We share this suffering. We feel an obligation to support those who have no rights and are oppressed. We believe that we have been sent to proclaim good news which makes everyone strong and confirms that the marginalized, too, are children of God. We attempt to relieve the suffering of those entrusted to us. Beyond dispute we are closer to the minority than to the majority. This limits our possibilities for action. We share in the tension between majority and minority. How can we love the ones and not hurt the others? We feel trapped in structural sins which have been handed down in a long tradition and ask how we can free ourselves from them. The church has shared our history. It has suffered with us. How can it cope with this responsibility?

Perhaps our fate and our problem does not fit in with modern thought. Why, it might be asked, take on the burden of a particular culture? That is almost incomprehensible against the background of the experience of pluralistic societies. A number of things could be said here. One does not carry a culture just as a fate or as a neutral object, but as that place in the world and its history where one really feels at home. The nation and history of one's own people define that Archimedean point from which one has a chance of changing the world. In pre-modern societies in particular the nation can be a very important part of identity. That is important. But in our area the key question lies elsewhere. If one is expelled and then meets others who have suffered the same fate, one quickly joins forces with them and attempts to share in coping with the constraints that have been imposed. The question of minorities is often constructed 'from above'. That is also the case with us.

I The oppression of minorities

There are many minorities. They are often defined by their ethno-social and linguistic characteristics. They only become a problem when 'minority' does not denote a quantitative relationship but a special social position. The minority can easily become the object of constraints. Even if otherwise all factors – cultural forces, economic capacity, social commitment – remain the same, its difference in magnitude is a disadvantage to the minority. There are burdens which are simply the consequences of lesser numbers. Others come from the greed of the stronger, who attack the weaker. The majority can also deliberately threaten the minority, so that they themselves can have more, or simply in order not to be disturbed.

The relative weakness of a minority exposes it to pressure towards assimilation. The majority controls and owns the institutions: education and the media, state administration and the greater part of public life, business and jobs. One has to move in a world of organizations which were created and developed by the majority and on which the minority has little influence. These are organizations which do not serve to preserve the values and characteristics of the minority and which make use of a language which is foreign to that minority. Already as a technical or organizational factor, the majority–minority relationship is a disadvantage to those who are numerically fewer. This is almost automatically associated with a social majorization. In buying and in trading, in interpersonal relationships with colleagues at work and neighbours, the minority is drawn into the undertow of the customs, ways of life, expectations of the majority. Even in seeking a partner there is a greater choice in the majority group than in the minority.

The majority dominates the cultural framework. It leaves its stamp on everyday culture. It decides what colours will dominate fashion and the streets. Its tradition shapes architecture and city planning. Its music resounds from countless loudspeakers, cars and pubs. Cuisine follows the majority taste. And of course this majority tries to make its character felt: with its own historiography, with national myths, with a cultural orientation, all of which are far from the self-understanding of the minority. The majority and the minority give different names to historical figures, to towns and villages. But only the majority has the power to establish its own version generally and officially. The dimensions of time and space, the whole country and all its history, are commandeered by the majority, independently of the existence, past and cultural achievements of the minority. The latter inevitably feel robbed.

The frontiers between majority and minority are often drawn by language. This marks out both groups and keeps them apart. The ruling group speaks differently from the 'common people', the subjects, or the minority understood in socio-political terms. Language and linguistic competence become qualifying criteria. A pressure is exercised from 'above' 'downwards'. What is called for is not multilingualism, but a perfect control of the language of the majority. A minority with a mother tongue which differs from that of the majority is at a disadvantage from the cradle on. A minority has to make an additional effort to keep up in linguistic terms, and has to fight against the constant erosion of its language. Some spheres of life are under the exclusive control of the ruling majority: professional life with its many technical terms, the modern spheres of culture where new terminology is only now becoming established, and not least the sphere of politics and the exercise of rule. The language of a minority threatens to become only the language of family and the tradition, not of public life or the shaping of the future.

The pressure exercised by the majority towards assimilation is a fact, regardless of its purposes. To limit it would require special efforts, a 'positive discrimination', the deliberate protection of minorities. This kind of action can only be expected where the majority regards the safeguarding of the minority and equal opportunities for it as a moral, cultural or social gain. All too often this is not the case. On the contrary! The majority often regards itself as the only criterion and is concerned to advance assimilation deliberately. Any special cultivation of the cultural (or other) characteristics of the majority is largely directed against the minority and suggests its inferiority. Who could doubt that the majority may legitimately draw attention to its own achievements, virtues, capacities and values? But what happens when the majority, precisely in its otherness which is distinct from the minority, claims to possess unique special qualities? This cultivation of values automatically turns into a confrontation in which the minority is judged inferior. This verdict presupposes a lack of qualities, of values, historical sinfulness and guilt. It is hard to avoid the construction of a complex of prejudice and resentment which arises in this way. Originally it is not rooted in the negative assessment of the minority but in the self-celebration of the majority. However, the comparison between the groups and cultures of the majority and the minority becomes an 'objective' basis for random discriminatory measures and demands.

The majority can feel that its hegemony and the undisturbed implementation of its cultural ideas is disrupted by the existence of the minority. It can also try to make it difficult, indeed impossible, for the minority to preserve its culture and independence and to communicate. A minority which has been robbed of its community and its possibilities for social expression will perish. Something dies in people along with their self-understanding. The slow death of the culture of a minority is tormenting for those concerned. This death can be hastened by a dispersion of the minority and by the opening up of their enclosed settlement areas. The state has the power to determine that, in the cities of the minorities, new buildings may only be lived in by members of the majority population. Or conversely, an authoritarian state can destroy villages and settle their inhabitants randomly in other towns. In a centralized state a mixture of races and cultures can be promoted by moving the work-force or fixing the location of jobs.

The majority not only has the state at its service. Churches, too, can become supporters of the national interest, especially where ethnic and confessional frontiers coincide. Again, churches can be built, dioceses established, seminaries founded, where no believers of a confession live. A church, a missionary and the pressure of the power and the majority and financial inducements and prospects of careers may make converts. At any rate such developments can break the cultural and religious unity of a minority. However, the means and the personnel for religious imperialism are not at the disposal of the minority.

The most public forms of discrimination, the withdrawal of legal rights or physical threats, are only the tip of the iceberg. Pehaps the language may be banned. More often the possibility of speaking it disappears altogether.

Occasionally the majority uses force to break the life-style and culture of the minority. But direct force is not necessary where the living conditions of the minority are determined by the majority. A civil war or the violent throttling of a minority, an ethnic group, a nationality are still exceptions. However, a minority can suffer and be suffocated silently in the stranglehold of the majority.

II Consequences and attempts at defence

Where a state people or a majority defines itself in national terms, the result is that that ethnic minority is forced out of the system of normal social competition. Perhaps the minority will succeed in discovering a gap in the system, in business or in finance. Perhaps the minority will be able to assert itself by its own economic and political social links, as is shown by the history of the Jews and the Armenians. But these are exceptions. Where the criteria of social evaluation are not established by neutral assessments of powers or competition and achievement but by the cultural preferences of the majority, a minority which has other characteristics, or whose capabilities are not recognized as being equal, must expect loss of status. For those who belong to the minority, the ways up the social ladder are made more difficult, perhaps even blocked.

A threatened status can then be a stimulus to look beyond the limits of a country or a nation. That is the opportunity for a mercantile class or a middle class with international links. Things look different with the frontiers of a land. The official culture can be dominated, monopolized by the majority. That leads to a constriction of the horizons of those without power, to a distortion of their awareness of history and to a burden on their openness to the future. Language, tradition, customs become inexpressive, weak. Cultural independence can only partially be preserved, and members of the minority have to come to terms with the slow loss of their social identity. Some emigrate. Many take the solution of abandoning their nationality. It is a leap into the unknown. No one knows whether he or she will be accepted by the majority. And at all events cutting oneself off from one's roots is painful. Nevertheless, some succeed in assimilating. But most are incapable of this. Perhaps they are too old, or not flexible enough. Perhaps they cannot separate from friends, relatives, their childhood and their children. They continue to bear the burden of their nationality. They may bear this proudly and defiantly. But underneath there is a good deal of self-deception. Discrimination and undervaluation are countered by a flight into imaginary worlds. The minority situation produces a distorted sense of reality in many people. The obstacles preventing access to some spheres of the dominant culture cause uncertainties. Powerlessness can issue in hopelessness. Many give up inside. They do not want any more children who have no future. Sometimes they do not even want to go on living. The demographic differences between the majority (Roumanian) and the minority (German, or Hungarian) are shocking in our country.

A group which has become aware of itself has a certain power of survival. A nationality spontaneously develops cultural and social defence mechanisms. Reflex protective measures are taken to cope with disadvantages and oppression. Is one's own culture endangered and undervalued? The minority is almost forced to glorify itself. To compensate, it reinforces its own cultural consciousness and embellishes its own culture. Does the majority erect insuperable barriers for its culture? In response the minority stops the contacts which are dangerous for it and attempts to preserve the purity of its own tradition. Similarly, a threatened group quite spontaneously strengthens its social connections. It moves into a ghetto. It attempts to prevent marriages, friendships, everyday contacts with 'others'. It rejects any mixing. However, the elevation of the internal unity of the ethnic, national, linguistic minority heightens the tension between the majority and the minority. When there is a sharper separation and the frontiers are clearer, each side can appeal to the intransigence of the other.

A minority and its members confronts an oppressive dilemma. They can assimilate unconditionally, and deny their history, their views and inclinations which have been shaped by history, indeed ultimately themselves. Wounds remain. These may perhaps have to be cauterized in order to make the change of worlds final and credible. However, this self-mutilation is not a way of human development. Another possibility is an attempt at self-assertion. The price for this is endless conflict, increasing discrimination and the harmful and crippling consequences of disadvantage. A minority always draws the short straw. In the nation state it is the loser. The worst thing is when the majority itself is struggling with identity difficulties and tries to overcome these by vilifying and destroying the minority. Then the minority is condemned to a slow death.

III Under the protection of religion and church

A persecuted group may be shown sympathy from many sides. However, hardly anyone can offer real hope. The last protection and comfort of a minority lies in religion. This provides four supports: as a cultural sphere, as the foundation of community, as a point of reference which is above earthly interests, and as a cry from the depths of the fate of a minority for the support of God and the church.

Religion is also a sphere, a treasure chamber of social memory. The houses of God are monuments of past self-understandings. They hand down the message of ancestors. Their symbolism has a language of its own. The saints, the statues, the pictures, the relics, the sacred objects represent the faith and the power of generations long dead. The liturgy, the festival customs, the hymns, the texts, the greetings, are testimonies and guardians of a cultural heritage. Prayers which one learned as a small child are lost only with death. Religion preserves the mother tongue – at least where there is prayer to God. Cultural memories are kept alive in religion, and the longing to perceive cultural and national identity strengthens the observance of religious tradition.

Religion is community and creates community. It is the communion of those who worship the same God. It is still tangibly the community of those people who call on and worship God in the same way, with similar words and expression. We pray 'Our Father . . .'. For most of us, this 'we', or 'our', is a tangible community, where we are accepted, where we are at home, which we feel to be ours. We can hardly understand anything else by 'we'. 'Our' God is often (wrongly) called on in this way. There is temptation to keep God in one's own culture, to use God as an instrument for the purposes of one's own survival, the danger of making God a national idol. The reason for this is our impotence, our inability to raise ourselves above our needs. But even in such a distorted form, religion remains an elemental community. A minority can lose its schools and public institutions. It can be forbidden to form a political association, or this can be made impossible. Its communality can be contested by the state as a destruction of national unity. But its religious roots remain.

Religion consolidates this-worldly ties like culture and community. That is of some importance. But the decisive factor lies elsewhere. Faith relativizes earthly distress. It recalls a wider human destiny. It conveys an identity which is above discrimination and persecution. It is the basis for a view of the world which is not burdened by social and cultural contradictions. It insists on the equality of all human beings, on the redemption of all who accept the universal invitation to be heirs of God. It restores the dignity which the majority has refused.

Faith is a personal decision. It calls for the acceptance of the neighbour and the healing of wounds. Thus it begins by supporting the wounded, those without power, those without independence. The Christian religion and the church call for the option for the weak. They embody support for the oppressed minority. But can polarization be avoided in this decision? Or does the church find itself in the maelstrom of tensions and battles between majority and minority, between ruling people and nationalities?

IV Beyond nationalism?

Some attempts are being made at avoiding entanglement in the dispute between races and groups. The Neo-Protestant sects are increasing rapidly. They can solve the problem by opting out of society. They proclaim a radically other-worldly doctrine. They repudiate the world. They consign the world and its tensions to the devil. They call for renunciation of the world. They create small counter-worlds for themselves. Their dualistic system is a solution for those who are in it. That may in part explain their successes. But this does not influence social conditions.

There are spiritual movements in the mainstream churches which in their own way contribute towards a solution. In movements like Focolare or the charismatic renewal, members of the majority and the minority, of this or that race and language, can meet together peacefully. These movements are establishing a pre-intellectual, pre-cultural human determination: humanity comes before nationality. In principle they are not uninterested in the social situation, but at most they can offer their view of their world, their joy in life and their unconditional brotherhood and sisterhood; they cannot make it a social norm and precept.

And what about the churches themselves? Of course they call for service and testimony. Self-denial and love of neighbour are prime values of Christianity. And the neighbour is not found in those who are known, those who belong, but in all those who are in need. However, unconditional love of neighbour is made difficult for the members of a minority by a small shift in accent. They are the ones who are humiliated and persecuted. They are opposing the actions, the nationalism, of the majority, a system which refuses human rights. This system is advocated not only by officials and cultural activitists, but by all those who assert the inferiority of the minority and put its rights and free existence in question. Would it be wrong to call for basic rights? Do the members of a minority have to renounce their identity for the sake of peace? Could they? And can they and may they call on their fellow citizens and children to renounce their identity? Would that be technically possible? Would it be morally right? The church has little left. It proclaims the duty to love one's neighbour, and forgiveness and reconciliation. But that does not stop it arguing for basic rights. And it puts itself on the side of those without rights. Perhaps it will therefore even become the target of the majority; but it cannot decide otherwise.

Countries and frontiers have changed often in Central Europe during the twentieth century. In the past there were ruling nations and also national minorities. There are now. In many cases those involved have changed. In some countries, nations which were leaders of history have become nationalities. Roles have been exchanged, but the basic situation has remained. The majorities are uncertain of themselves and want to assert themselves in the European balance of power. Therefore they appeal to the national element. That is why they are seeking ethnic, linguistic and national homogeneity. That is why they are attempting to deal with national minorities or to assimilate them. And the minorities are fighting against discrimination. They are attempting to reinforce their cohesion, their own culture, their own national disposition. The majority regards the minority as a threat to the national identity and unity of which it dreams. But the minority regards the dreams and and the concrete measures of the majority as a threat to its rights and its existence. The opposition is complete. Both sides have an excuse for their actions directed against the other side. Their own actions are always only protective measures, and attacks are justified as preventing a great evil. Mutual suspicion, re-criminations and violation are now the order of the day. There is a seamless system of structural sin. One is entangled in it if one is born here or even if one wants to help here.

Their demographic and also historical links with each of the nations is a burden on the churches. To take our example: the Roumanians are for the most part members of the Orthodox Church. A minority belongs to the Greek Catholic, i.e. Uniate Catholic, Church with the Byzantine rite. The Germans are for the most part Catholic, but some are Protestants. The Hungarians are half Catholic and half Protestant. The Orthodox claim to be the 'national' church. The state tends to regard all the other churches as the agents of the unpopular minorities (or of their motherlands, or even of the Vatican).

National differences have detrimental consequences for the churches. Their hands are politically tied in many respects. However, the manifest difficulties in no way diminish the obligation to mediate and seek a solution. Particularly within the church nothing must stand in the way of understanding. Yet reality looks different. Catholic bishops have cool relations with the majority language and with the minority languages. In the eastern half of the country the use of the Hungarian minority language is forbidden by the bishop in the liturgy and even in the confessional.

Priests with the minority language may not even work there. (The hymns and prayers of great processions to non-Roumanian places of pilgrimages are eloquent testimony to the need for a non-Roumanian liturgy.)

Perhaps here we have temporary inconsistencies. However, it is an abiding fact that the church has no institutions for national dialogue, for understanding within the church, for fighting the excesses of nationalism. This does not seem to be a special feature of our country. But for many reasons it should not be the case. By virtue of their cultural and social role, the churches are not free of all blame in the origin of the structural sin which has developed with nationalism. They were (or are) part of that political development in which nationalism was formed. Their guilt is coupled with their present involvement. They, too, are damaged by nationalism. Thirdly, they have their task of reconciliation. Their self-understanding requires them to be a 'sacrament, that is a sign and instrument . . . for the unity of all humankind' (*Lumen gentium* 1). Finally, one argument comes from the international political situation. The world seems in many conflicts, bloody and bloodless, to be looking for mediators who are not pursuing their own interests, and are not just content with the ploys of the pragmatic balance of power. There are high expectations of the churches. But first of all the church must prove its willingness and capability by an inner dialogue.

The human dignity of national minorities and a social and cultural milieu in which this dignity can be cultivated has been and is supported successfully by the churches. That is one side of the coin. A national reconciliation and a demolition of nationalistic hostilities is also needed to make possible full human development and participation in the life of society with equal rights, and also to take the poison out of existing conflicts. But so far few systematic efforts have been made in this direction. That is the other side. The message of Christ and the well-being of the nations also calls for more consistent efforts in the second sphere.

Translated by John Bowden

Notes

1. These are pseudonyms; the names of the contributors are known to the editors.

IV · Religion and Nationalism World-Wide

What Kind of Nationalism? Ethical Distinctions

Gregory Baum

There are many kinds of nationalism. Among the attempts to find an appropriate classification for them, I prefer that which distinguishes between two different political functions exercised by them, even if these functions sometimes overlap. There are nationalisms that struggle against the feudal–aristocratic and later the imperialist–colonial order to construct and sustain a modern citizenship state; and there are nationalisms that lament the cultural impact of modernity and want industrial society to return to its ethnic, cultural or religious roots. What interests me in this article are thinkers who have reflected on nationalisms in moral terms and set down ethical norms to distinguish between morally-acceptable and morally-unacceptable forms of nationalism. Most of these thinkers have been religious personalities. In this article I wish to summarize the ideas of three such thinkers, Martin Buber, Mahatma Gandhi and Paul Tillich.[1]

Martin Buber

1. Martin Buber offered two different theories of nationalism. As a young man, writing prior to World War I, Buber was an ardent critic of modernity.[2] He held a position shared by many sociologists, philosophers and religious thinkers that modern society was undermining traditional values and institutions. Symptomatic of this trend was Ferdinand Tönnies' *Gemeinschaft und Gesellschaft*[3] (1887), which offered a sociological analysis of the difference between traditional and modern society and which could be read as a lament over the loss of roots, the breakdown of community, the spread of individualism, the decline of culture and the death of idealism. At the turn of the century we witness nationalist

movements in many European societies advocating a return to the roots of culture and the recovery of a sense of community.

Buber shared the position that modern society alienated people from their roots. Europeans, he argued, were working and living in institutions that did not reflect their deepest values and thus estranged them from their moral ground. To live authentically and transcend the internal split, people had to return to their roots and recreate their societies accordingly. The alienation of modern Jews, Buber argued, was simply a more intense example of the estrangement experienced by other Europeans.

Jews worked and lived in the institutions of their host countries, cut off from the values and ideals of their Hebrew roots. They were worse off than people of other nations because they, the Jews, did not have a land on which to create their own public institutions. Buber tells us that his encounter with Zionism in 1903 – the movement had been founded by Herzl in 1897 – was experienced by him as the beginning of his liberation. He believed that in Zion, his people would be able to create institutions that reflected the Hebrew spirit and live their daily lives in keeping with their deepest aspirations.

Buber looked with approval at nationalist movements in other countries that resisted the superficiality of modern life and called for the conversion to the depth of culture. He was critical of Herzl's perception of Zionism since he, the founder of the movement, tried to promote it by political and diplomatic means and did not call for the conversion of the Jews to their spiritual roots. Buber had more sympathy for Ahad Ha'am, the Eastern European Zionist leader, who envisaged a transformed, biblically-inspired Hebrew culture in the promised land, transcending the values of bourgeois society. But since Ha'am was a secularist and since his biblically-based Hebrew society left no place for the Eternal, Buber could not agree with him. The only kind of Jewish nationalism acceptable to Buber was one that was ruled by Prophetic Judaism, that is to say the religion of the classical Hebrew prophets, which consisted of trust and faith in the Eternal and dedication to justice, compassion and peace. Buber insisted that a radical conversion to this prophetic faith was required of Orthodox and Reformed Jews, because – according to him – the former were preoccupied with observance and hence were locked in the past, and the latter trivialized the Jewish tradition and thus encouraged assimilation.

At this stage, Buber advocated nationalism as the entry into personal authenticity. He offered an existentialist justification of nationalism. It seems curious to the contemporary reader that Buber made only brief references to the possibility that nationalist movements could lead to collective arrogance, intolerance to minorities, hostility to outsiders, a sense of cultural superiority, or even to the elevation of the nation as the highest value. Buber regarded nationalism as a movement grounded in aspirations that were essentially ethical. For Jews, he thought, this ethos was rooted in Prophetic Judaism.

2. After World War II, Martin Buber offered an anthropological justification of nationalism.[4] Arguing against an individualistic understanding of the human person, he proposed that persons come to be through interaction with parents and their community and through an identification with a language, a culture and a history. Buber strongly believed in the unity of humanity created by God, but he argued that people are integrated into humanity not as individuals but as members of a community. A community becomes a people or a nation when the major events that shape its history are honoured and remembered and produce a sense of common destiny that distinguishes it from other peoples or nations. While the early Buber interpreted the nation in terms of ethnic continuity, he now regards peoplehood as historically constructed by the memory of common experiences, a common interpretation of history and a sense of solidarity and joint responsibility. Such a people is ethically entitled to create its own political, social and cultural institutions. Buber applied this rule to all peoples – to Jews as well as to Palestinians.

At this stage, Buber was more sensitive to the dangers implicit in nationalist movements. He argued that the sense of nationhood arises in special moments of social and political crisis when a collectivity becomes aware of a deficiency in its social existence, such as the lack of land or territorial security, the lack of freedom to create to its own political life, or the absence of an effective unity. 'In a healthy nation, nationalism will recede as the deficiency is corrected. In an unhealthy nation, however, nationalism exceeds its rightful limits and becomes a permanent principle. In this situation, nationalism is no longer a response to a disease but is itself a great and complicated disease.'[5] As long as the nation is not elevated to an end in itself, nationalism may still continue to be fruitful. However, 'the moment national ideology makes the nation an end in itself, it annuls its own right to live'.

Exploring his second interpretation of nationalism, Buber retained his religious and ethical passion. A nation, he insisted, must serve the unity of the human family. Any form of nationalism that encourages claims of national superiority over others or generates cultural contempt for others was evil. When he moved to Palestine in the late 1930s, he supported the right of self-determination for Jews and for Palestinians. After the foundation of the State of Israel, he was critical of the official Zionism sponsored by the government and remained a faithful witness to the spirit of Prophetic Judaism.

Mahatma Gandhi

Mahatma Gandhi understood Hindu nationalism primarily as a call to personal conversion. In his pamphlet of 1909, 'Hind Swaraj' (Indian Self-rule),[6] he offered a radical statement of his spiritual and political programme, which he never revoked. It announced the total rejection of Western civilization, symbolized by British society, whose highest value – Gandhi believed – was bodily welfare, i.e. the acquisition of wealth and comfort. 'If India copies England, it is my firm conviction that she will be ruined.'[7] This state of affairs, he continued, is not due to any particular fault of the English; it is due rather to modern, Western civilization. The English are to be pitied, he wrote, because they have been cut off from their roots and made to betray their ethical tradition. They have been made over by modernity. They now misconceive the nature of human being and entertain a false view of life's meaning.

We find in this pamphlet a critique of modernity that pushes Ferdinand Tönnies to an extreme. Modernity makes people into individualists, materialists, secularists and utilitarians engaged in a frantic search for the happiness that material things can offer, yet ironically prevented from ever finding even that happiness.

Indian self-rule (swaraj) therefore means primarily personal conversion, that is the soul's rule over one's personal life. Gandhi tells us that India has a spiritual tradition that communicates self-rule. The people in Indian villages that have not been touched by British power and influence enjoy self-rule: they have been taught to possess their soul, they live the good life in modesty, gentleness, love of neighbour, and openness to the sacred. But because of British domination, self-rule (swaraj) has come to mean more: it now means self-government in a political sense, freedom from British power and influence, and the creation of an Indian state.

Gandhi was critical of the existing nationalist movements in India.[8] 'The moderates' wrestled for Indian sovereignty in reliance on British legal institutions; they repudiated violence and sought the support of Liberals and Labourites in Britain. 'The radicals' turned to Hinduism as the bond that united the great majority of Indians and resisted British institutions, often making use of violence. Gandhi rejected the gradualism and assimilationism of the moderates, even though he shared their horror of violence. He agreed with the radicals in their turn to Hindu religion and the repudiation of British institutions, but he rejected their use of violence and their unwillingness to compromise and seek interim solutions. Gandhi believed that Indian nationalism was ethical only when it conformed to the spirituality of India's religions, Hinduism and Islam,[9] interpreted in terms of the Hindu tradition of non-violence or truth-force (satyagraha) and of special solidarity with the poor. Gandhi shocked the moderate and the radical nationalists, largely elite groups of educated Indians, when he proposed to purify the Hindu idea of untouchability and integrate the so-called untouchables as equal citizens into Indian society.

Of interest to us is the famous debate over nationalism between Gandhi and the Indian poet, Tagore.[10] Tagore was a Hindu with a universalist philosophy. He believed that at the core of all religions was a yearning for justice and peace and a hope for a reconciled humanity. He also saw positive elements in secular Western culture. He admired the West for its intellectual and scientific dynamism and for its culture of lawfulness, promoting both lawful behaviour and equality before the law. He called this 'the spirit of the West'. But witnessing the brutalities of World War I, he became a strong opponent of nationalism. While he greatly admired Gandhi's personal sanctity, he repudiated Gandhi's nationalism, especially in 1923 when Gandhi organized a movement of non-cooperation with the British, rejecting not only British education and the English language but also British-made products, especially textiles. Gandhi asked the people to return to the spinning wheel and the hand loom, and make their own clothes. Tagore, shocked by Gandhi's campaign of 'spin and weave', published an attack on Gandhi's ideas and a denunciation of nationalism.

Tagore praised what he called the spirit of the West and condemned the nation of the West, i.e. the nationalisms that had created the modern state and produced a climate of competition among the nations. The nation of the West, he argued, was hostile to the spirit of the West: dedication to truth-seeking and science and commitment to equality and lawful behaviour were undermined and destroyed by the nationalisms of the West. According to Tagore, Gandhi made the great mistake of rejecting the West in its entirety, including the spirit of the West, while adopting quite inconsistently the nation of the West, that is to say the deadly nationalism. The campaign of non-cooperation and the call 'spin and weave', Tagore argued, revealed that Gandhi's nationalism impoverished the Indian tradition which favoured co-operation and which called people not so much to material things, 'spin and weave', but to deepen their spiritual life. Self-rule, Tagore argued, is practised in people's personal lives; there is no need to follow the West in organizing a nationalist movement aiming at the formation of a modern state.

Gandhi defended his nationalist cause. He admitted that he was not fully comfortable with the idea of a modern state; he admitted – as we have seen – that self-rule was first of all a personal conversion; he admitted, moreover, that there were many dangers associated with the formation of a state, yet he justified his struggle for political self-rule and the creation of an Indian state in terms of his compassionate identification with the poor and destitute of the Indian subcontinent. Only a sovereign state, he believed, had the power to intervene, redistribute the wealth of country and rescue the many millions from their misery. To achieve social transformation, including the reform of the Hindu tradition, the state was, alas, a necessary instrument. The conversion of the heart was not enough; it had to be accompanied by an anti-colonial struggle for Indian self-rule.

Paul Tillich

Paul Tillich belonged to the few anti-Fascist writers of the 1930s who had sympathy for people's search for roots.[11] He thought that liberals and socialists, especially Marxists, misunderstood the nature of nationalism. Since liberals looked upon human beings as rational agents seeking to increase their material advantage, they thought that nationalists were sentimentally attached to the past, to the detriment of their rational self-interest. And since Marxists thought that human beings were destined by history to serve the material interest of their economic class, they argued that proletarians had no fatherland and that nationalism was a form of false consciousness. Arguing against them, Tillich offered an anthropological argument to show the importance of roots in people's lives, whether these roots be national, cultural, ethnic or religious. (Tillich was well acquainted with Martin Buber: in the 1920s in Germany they belonged to the same circle of religious socialists.)

Tillich explained what he called the powers of origin. Rootedness, he argued, generates 'eros' and 'fate'. By 'eros' he meant the love of family, the attachment to home and home country, the spontaneous solidarity with one's community, and the emotional bond to the cultural inheritance encountered in childhood. And by 'fate' he meant the profound sense that one belonged to a community, remembered the same events, suffered from the same defeats and shared a common destiny. Eros and fate, according to Tillich, were the sources of human passion and human creativity: through them, through their roots, people were linked to their vital, creative energies.

Tillich argued that liberalism and socialism, in virtue of their excessive rationalism, tried to detached people from their roots and thereby limited their access to the forces of life. They undermined human vitality. At the same time Tillich recognized the dangers created by a political philosophy that was solely based on the return to roots or, as he called it, guided by a myth of origin. Such a political orientation would create a strong distinction between 'us' and 'them', a sense of superiority of 'us' over 'them', an attitude that would eventually lead to aggression and war. A political philosophy based wholly on the powers of origin also mediated into the present the hierarchical subordinations inherited from the past, masters over servants, men over women, owners over workers, and so forth, leading inevitably to discrimination and oppression. Writing in 1932, Tillich predicted that if the Nazis assumed power in Germany this would destroy Germany and threaten the entire European civilization.

While Tillich defended the return to roots and therefore had sympathy with nationalism, he believed that a nationalist movement had to be strictly subordinated to social justice. But where did such a call to justice come from? This call was mediated by what Tillich called a myth of demand, a secular myth of the just society created by the liberal or socialist enlightenment, grounded – Tillich believed – in God's promises to Israel and the unconditional demand proclaimed by classical Hebrew prophecy. In his terminology, a myth of origin must be broken or refracted by a myth of unconditional demand.

Tillich, the theologian, pointed to the Exodus, the story of divine rescue, as the myth of origin that guided the people of Israel and their kings, and to classical Hebrew prophecy as providing the myth of demand that refracted Israel's reliance on its election. The prophets preached that it was not enough to belong to the covenanted people or be their anointed king; what God demanded was justice for the poor – the orphan, the widow and the stranger. Here the myth of origin was refracted by the myth of unconditional demand. But the message of the prophets was not a foreign word to the Israelites, since the yearning for justice was already present in the covenant God had made with the people.

Tillich, the socialist, held that in the modern, secular society it was socialism that mediated the unconditional demand. He shared the opinion of such authors as Ernst Bloch and Karl Mannheim that the socialist, egalitarian imagination in Western society was derived from the biblical prophetic tradition. The great mistake that socialism had made, according to Tillich, was that it undermined people's attachment to their roots. The reason that the ordinary people in the country and in small towns did not vote for socialism, even though this would have been to their economic benefit, was that they loved their roots, their local community and their religion and recognized that socialism had no respect for these.

Marxism, Tillich argued, was imprisoned in bourgeois rationalism. The rationalist misconception of Marxism was the idea that working people joined the socialist revolution because they were driven by history to enhance the rational interest of their class. Workers indeed want to improve the material conditions of their lives, but this – according to Tillich – is not the main reason for their socialist commitment. Workers are not as alienated from their culture and their human substance as Marxist theory claims. Workers love their wives and children, have warm feelings for their local community, enjoy their landscape, and remain attached to their cultural and possibly their religious roots: and they realize that all this is threatened by the negative, cultural impact of industrial capitalism. The loss of community, denounced by Tönnies and other social critics, is felt by ordinary working people. Hence their commitment to socialism, Tillich argued, is grounded in the attachment to their origin, i.e. in a non-rational factor. Socialism will be able to escape bourgeois rationalism when it learns to respect people's love of their national, ethnic and religious roots, and at the same time subordinate these vital forces to the unconditional demand of justice, equality and peace.

This brief account of their social philosophies allows us to conclude that Gandhi and Buber offered an ethical justification of nationalism. For these religious thinkers, nationalism was a spiritual way calling for conversion before it was a political movement seeking the establishment of a state. They believed that if the nationalist movement they supported should deviate from the ethical norms derived from its religious tradition, Hindu or Jewish, it would become a dangerous political force generating arrogance, hostility, injustice and war. Gandhi justified this risk because he thought it was the only way to help the masses of the poor. Buber justified the risk because he believed that the establishment of the Jewish nation in Zion was in accordance with the divine promises. Tillich, who did not think of himself as a nationalist, believed that the contempt of nationalism was as much an error as the uncritical surrender to it. While he valued the return to historical roots as a source of human creativity, he realized the potential of this return to become a force of oppression and aggression. He therefore demanded that a turning to the powers of national, ethnic or religious origin be strictly subordinated to the unconditional demand of justice and peace. Gandhi, Buber and Tillich were egalitarians. They advocated an egalitarian economy beyond capitalism: Gandhi favoured an austere, co-operative village economy extended over the whole of India, Buber supported an ethically-grounded, decentralizing socialism, and Tillich writing in Germany prior to 1933 entertained an explicit, revisionist Marxist perspective.

Notes

1. In a more detailed study I also examine the thought of the French Catholic thinker and poet, Charles Péguy, the Quebec Catholic social theologian, Jacques Grand'maison, and the French Jewish philosopher, Emmanuel Lévinas.

2. See Buber's 'Three Speeches on Judaism', given between 1909 and 1911 in Prague, published in English translation in Martin Buber, *On Judaism*, ed. N. N. Glatzer, New York 1967. See also Laurence Silberstein, *Martin Buber's Social and Religious Thought*, New York 1989, and Maurice Friedman, *Encounter on the Narrow Ridge: A Life of Martin Buber*, New York 1991.

3. See the English translation, F. Tönnies, *Community and Society*, East Lansing, MI 1987.

4. See Martin Buber, *Israel and the World: Essays in a Time of Crisis*, New York 1948.

5. Ibid., 218.

6. For the important sections of 'Hind Swaraj', see *Sources of Indian Tradition*, ed. W. Theodore de Bary, Vol. II, New York 1968, 251–67.

7. Ibid., 251.

8. For an analysis of the forms of Indian nationalism prior to Gandhi, see ibid., 108–86.

9. For the care Gandhi took to include the Muslim tradition, see Sheila McDonaugh, *Gandhi's Response to Islam*, New Delhi 1994.

10. For the texts of this debate, see *Sources of Indian Tradition* (n.6), 230–74.

11. Tillich's analysis is found in his brilliant *Die sozialistische Entscheidung* (1933), published in English translation as *The Socialist Decision*, New York 1977.

Secularism, Hindu Nationalism and the Fear of People

Ashis Nandy

The paradox of secularism

Secularism as an ideology thrives in societies that are predominantly non-secular. Once a society begins to get secularized – that is, once it is increasingly cleansed of religion and ideas of transcendence – the political status of secularism changes. In such a society, people become aware of living in an increasingly desacralized world and begin to search for faiths, to give meaning to their life and retain the illusion of being part of a traditional community. If faiths are in decline, they begin to look for ideologies linked to faiths, in an effort symbolically to return to traditions that would negate or defy the world in which they live.

When Indian public life was predominantly non-modern, secularism as an ideology had a chance. For the area of the sacred looked intact and safe, and secularism looked like a balancing principle and a form of dissent. Even many believers who flaunted their faith in public described themselves as secular, to keep up with the times and because secularism sounded like something vaguely good. Now that the secularization of Indian polity has gone far, the appeal of secularism has declined. For signs of secularization are now everywhere: one does not have to make a case for it. Instead, the fear has grown that the decline in public morality in the country is due to the all-round decline in religious sensibilities. Many distorted or perverted versions of religion circulating in modern or semi-modern India owe their origins to this perception of the triumph of secularization rather than to that of traditions.

Many 'non-secular' ideologies and movements, too, have become more secular in content. They pretend to be otherwise, for the sake of their constituency, but they can pursue political power in a secularized polity only through secular politics, secular organizations and secular planning. They increasingly resemble the jet-setting gurus and sadhus who, while criticizing the 'crass materialism of the West', have to use Western technology, Western media and Western disciples at every step to stay in business. A popular formulation of this in India is that hypocritical politicians misuse religion. But it fails to acknowledge that only one who repudiates the sanctity of faiths can 'misuse' them or deploy them instrumentally.

Even riots or pogroms organized in the name of religion are becoming secular in South Asia. They are organized the way a rally or a strike is organized in a competitive, democratic polity, and usually for the same reasons – to bring down a regime or discredit a chief minister here or to help an election campaign or a faction there. Some political parties in India today have 'professionals' who specialize in such violence and do an expert job of it. Often these professionals, belonging to different religious or ethnic communities, maintain excellent social relationships with each other. Fanaticism, they seem to believe, is for the *hoi polloi*, not for serious polticians playing the game of ethnic politics. It is easy to find out the rate at which riots of various kinds can be bought, how political protection can be obtained for the rioters and how, after a riot, political advantage can be taken of it.

There is also a vague consensus among important sections of politicians, bureaucracy and mass media in South Asia on how such professionals should be treated – despite thousands of witnesses and detailed information, hardly anyone has been prosecuted for complicity in riots till now. The anti-Sikh pogrom in Delhi in 1984 is a case in point. It does not need much political acumen to predict that the same bright future awaits the organizers of the anti-Muslim pogrom in Bombay in January 1993.

Though by now human rights activists and students of violence have provided enough data to show that religious violence is mostly organized,[1] they have rarely pushed this point to its logical conclusion: that riots have to be organized because the ordinary citizens – the so-called illiterate, superstitious Indians – are not easy to rouse to participate in riots. To achieve that end, you need detailed planning and hard work. The ordinary citizens may not be epitomes of virtue, but they are not given to blood-curdling Satanism either. Not even when lofty modern values like history, state and nationalism are invoked. Their loves and hates are usually small-scale. In the case of religious violence, the most one can accuse them of is a certain uncritical openness to the rumours floated before riots, which help them make peace with their conscience and their inability to resist the violence.

Yet, they do resist. Each riot produces instances of bravery shown by persons who protect their neighbours at immense risk to their own lives and to those of their families.[2] The loves and hates of everyday life, which usually include ethnic and religious prejudices and stereotypes, are petty but not murderous. The resistance is stronger where communities have not splintered into atomized individuals. Riots are infrequent and harder to organize in villages.[3] The village community is breaking down all over the world, but it has not broken down entirely in South Asia. It is no accident that, despite the claim of some Hindu nationalists that more than 350,000 Hindus have already died fighting for the liberation of the Ramjanmabhumi during the last 400 years, the residents of Ayodhya themselves lived in reasonable amity till the late 1980s. The Hindu nationalists sensed this: till the mid-1980s, the case for demolishing the Babri mosque was not raised by any of its more noted leaders, from V. D. Savarkar and Keshav Hegdewar to Bal Thackeray and L. K. Advani. The issue was raised only after the Indian middle class attained a certain size and India's modernization reached a certain stage.

The first serious riot in the sacred city of Ayodhya took place on 6–7 December 1992. For seven years, despite all efforts to mobilize the locals for a riot, it had not taken place. This time, it was organized by outsiders and executed by non-Hindi-speaking rioters with whom the local Hindus could not communicate. These outsiders were not traditional villagers, but urbanized, semi-educated, partly Westernized men. They broke more than a hundred places of worship of the Muslims in the sacred city, to celebrate the 'fall' of the unprotected Babri mosque.[4]

The demolition of the Babri mosque at Ayodhya was not merely an attack on Hindu traditions, it was also a proof that the secularization of India had gone along predictable lines.

The fate of secularism

Whatever might have been once the contributions of secularism to Indian politics, institutionalized secularism now has begun to deliver less and less. Religious violence has grown more than ten-fold and has now begun to spread to rural India.[5] In the meanwhile, modern India has lost much of its faith in – and access to – the traditional social and psychological checks against religious violence.

The concept of secularism was imported into Indian public life as a replacement for the traditional concepts of inter-religious understanding and tolerance that had allowed thousands – yes, literally thousands – of communities living in the subcontinent to co-survive in neighbourliness. That co-survival was not easy or painless. Often there were violent clashes among the communities. But the violence never involved such large aggregates or generic categories as Hindus, Muslims or Sikhs. Conflicts were localized and cut across religious boundaries, for such boundaries were mostly fuzzy;[6] some of the clashes between sects, denominations and ethnicities have in retrospect begun to look like clashes between entire religious communities, and the religions in the region have begun to look complicit in that violence.

The traditional categories that sustained inter-religious accommodations, and contained communal animosities within tolerable limits, were systematically devalued as markers of native atavism. In their place, a modern state and the idea of secularism came to be seen as *the* solution to all inter-religious conflicts that had reportedly characterized the Indian society from ancient times. 'Reportedly', because no one produced an iota of evidence to show that such conflicts existed on a large scale and involved religious communities as they are presently defined. But modern Indians seemed convinced that the data did not exist because Indians did not have proper history, and had a scientific history existed, it would have shown that pre-modern India was a snake-pit of religious bigotry and cruelties.

The model worked as long as the Indian polity was characterized by a low level of politicization and collective violence was personalized, impassioned and irrational.[7] Politicization has grown, and ethnic and religious violence today is becoming more impersonal, organized, rational and calculative. The people who today provoke or participate in communal frenzy guided by secular political cost calculations do have an ideology apparently based on faith. But on closer scrutiny it turns out to be only secularized, arbitrarily chosen elements of faith. Institutionalized secularism, too, has in the meanwhile become ethnocidal and chronically dependent on the mercies of those controlling the state. Its domination has pushed other codes of religious and ethnic accommodation closer to extinction. So much so that religion as the cultural foundation for the existence of South Asian communities has increasingly become a feature of the poor, the weak and the rural.

With the decline of secularism have come new anxieties. Modern India, which now sets the tone of the culture of the Indian state, has begun to fear religion even more. That fear, part of a more pervasive fear of democracy which empowers the majority of Indians who are believers, has thrown up the various packaged forms of faith for the alienated Indians who populate urban, partly decultured India. These forms relegitimize garbled or tamed versions of religions catering to the needs of modern life, contain the fear of religions that are not centrally controllable (which often is a fear of the vernacular and the plural), and give their consumers the feeling that they have reconciled the old and the new, and the private and the public, in a creative fashion.

This is the challenge that Hindu nationalism has posed to Hinduism.

Hindu nationalism and the future of Hinduism

When a secularizing society throws up its own version of a faith, to cope with the changing psychological and cultural needs of the citizenry, the relationship between the new ideology and the old faith is bound to become ambivalent. Certainly the relationship between Hindutva, the ideology that inspires all Hindu nationalist movements and Hinduism, the faith that binds together a majority of Indians and scaffolds Indian culture, has been consistently tense or hostile outside the perimeters of urban India.

The reasons are obvious; the directions in which Hindu nationalism pushes Hinduism looks alien to most Hindus. For them, Hinduism is the faith by which they live. Hindutva is the ideology of mainly the upper-caste, middle-class, urban Indians uprooted from their culture.[8] Hindutva cannot but look like an attempt to protect, within Hinduism, the flanks of a consciousness which the democratic process threatens to corner.

That consciousness has two targets: the ordinary Hindus, seen as disorganized, faction-ridden, effeminate, superstitious and apolitical, and the aggressive minorities, mainly Muslims but also Christians, viewed as proselytizing, masculine, well-organized and united. The project is not only to exclude, resist or exile the followers of the semitic faiths who would not accept Hindu dominance, but also to win parity for the Hindus and to engineer them into respectable followers of semiticized Hinduism.[9] Hindutva is heir to the tenets and traditions of the nineteenth-century reform movements within Hinduism: it has to see Hinduism as inferior to the semitic creeds – monolithic, well-defined, self-aware and capable of being a sustaining ideology for an imperial state. Underlying both the projects is anger. It is the anger of Indians who have uprooted themselves from traditions, seduced by the promises of Indian modernity, and who now feel abandoned and humiliated. For many lower-middle-class, first-generation urban Indians, Indian modernization – especially that sub-category of it which goes by the name of developed – has failed. They have found easy scapegoats in the Muslims for this betrayal.

Hindutva is also sometimes the battle cry of lower-middle classes trying to break into the higher echelons of modern India (the Brahminic and classical components of the ideology are important from this point of view) and fearful that they may be driven into the ranks of the urban proletariat by the upper-caste, modern elite and the 'pushy' entrepreneurial classes from among the minorities (the urban concentration and artisan caste affiliations of a majority of the Muslims becomes important from this point of view). The contradiction showed in the temple movement culminating in the destruction of the Babri mosque in 1992. As heir to the nineteenth-century reform movements, Hindu nationalism is anti-idolatrous; as a political formation expressing the self-hatred and anger of the lower middle classes, it had to invoke Rama as a popular deity.

If Hindutva succeeds, Hinduism may not remain the faith of a majority of Indians. It will survive in pockets, cut off from the majority who will claim to live by it. Hindutva at this plane may turn out to be Western colonialism's last posthumous attack on Hinduism. That death of Hinduism will not be a source of sorrow for the votaries of Hindutva. For they have all along felt embarrassed by everyday Hinduism and wanted to turn it into an ideology meant for the supermarket of global mass culture where all religions are availbale in their consumerable forms, neatly packaged for the buyers.

Hindu nationalism, however, has its territorial limits. It cannot spread easily beyond the boundaries of urban, semi-Westernized India. It cannot easily penetrate South India, where Hinduism is more resilient and the Muslims do not invite the projection of the feared, unacceptable parts of one's own self. Nor can Hindutva survive where the citizens have not been massified and do not speak only the language of the state. That is why the Hindu nationalists have never tried to kill anyone among independent India's modern leadership: they killed the notorious counter-modernist – M. K. Gandhi. After the assassination, Jawaharlal Nehru claimed that the killer was insane. The modernist prime minister found it too painful to accept that Godse *was* sane, that he knew the real enemy of Hindutva.[10]

To those who live in Hinduism, Hindutva is one of those pathologies which periodically afflict a faith. Hinduism has, over the centuries, handled many such pathologies; it retains the capacity to handle one more. After all, has not Hinduism coped successfully with the West for the last two hundred years? If Hinduism triumphs, it may reduce Hindutva to its original status as a fringe phenomenon and offer the modern Hindus alternative psychological defences against the encroachment of the market, the state, and the urban-industrial vision. Hindutva, nineteenth-century imperialism's lost child, may then die a natural political death. But then it is also possible that that death will not be as natural as that of some other ideologies important at present; perhaps post-Gandhian Hinduism will have to take advantage of the democratic process to help Hindutva make a slightly inglorious exit from the South Asian stage.

Notes

1. E.g. Asghar Ali Engineer (ed.), *Communal Riots in Post-Independence India*, Hyderabad 1991.

2. E.g. Tariq Hasan, 'How Does it Matter Who is the Victim?', *The Times of India*, 3 April 1995.

3. Ashis Nandy, Shikha Trivedi, Shail Mayaram and Achyut Yagnik, *Creating a Nationality: The Ramjanmabhumi Movement and the Fear of the Self*, New Delhi 1995, ch. 1.

4. Ibid.

5. Ibid., ch. 1.

6. K. Suresh Singh, *Peoples of India*, Calcutta 1992, Vol. 1; Ashis Nandy, 'The Anti-Secularist Manifesto', *Seminar* 314, October 1985, 14–24; Gyanendra Pandev, *The Construction of Communalism in Colonial North India*, New Delhi 1990.

7. Ashis Nandy, 'The Politics of Secularism and the Recovery of Religious Tolerance', *Alternatives* 13.3, 1988, 177–94.

8. Clues to the cultural and psychological origins of Hinduism are in Walter K. Anderson and Sridhar D. Damle, *The Brotherhood in Saffron: The Rashtriya Swayamsevak Sangh and Hindu Revivalism*, New Delhi 1987; also Nandy et al., *The Ramjanmabhumi Movement* (n.3).

9. Nandy et al., *The Ramjanmabhumi Movement* (n.3).

10. Ashis Nandy, 'Final Encounter: The Politics of the Assassination of Gandhi', in *At the Edge of Psychology: Essays in Politics and Culture*, New Delhi 1980, 70–98.

Islam and Nationalism

Ziauddin Sardar

Islam and nationalism are contradictory terms. While Islam is intrinsically a universal creed and world-view which recognizes no geographical boundaries, nationalism is based on territory and is parochial in its outlook. While Islam insists on the total equality of humanity and recognizes no linguistic, cultural or racial barriers, nationalism glorifies assumed cultural, linguistic and racial superiority. Nationalism demands the total loyalty of a people to the nation ('my country, right or wrong'); Islam demands loyalty and submission only to God. Nationalism has given rise to the structure of the modern, sovereign nation-state which demands the promotion of its own interests in preference to, and at the cost of, all others; Islam, on the other hand, is uncompromising on the fact that sovereignty belongs only to God and it is His will, and not some perceived national interest, which should reign supreme in the world.

However, while Islam rejects the ideology of nationalism, it accepts both the existence of nations and the practice of nationhood. As the Qur'an declares: 'O Humanity! Behold, We have created you all out of a male and a female, and have made you into nations and tribes, so that you may recognize one another (not that you may despise one another)' (49.13). 'Nations and tribes' function as the providers of identity and thus lay the foundations of plurality in Islam. The basic social unit in Islam is the community, which functions both at a local and an international level. The local community is the neighborhood, gathered around a neighborhood mosque; the next level is the city community gathered around the Juma (or Friday) mosque; and the final level is the international network of communities of believers, the *ummah*, which is focused around the Sacred Mosque in Makkah. Thus while nations and tribes are recognized in Islam as part of the community, nationalism and tribalism are not; and the basic unit of an Islamic polity is not the nation, or the nation state, but the community.

But community in Islam is not some sort of romantic ideal that descends ready-made from heaven. Islam is not a passive religion: it asks its followers to be actively involved in shaping a Muslim community. To witness the *shahadah*, that is the fundamental declaration of Islam that 'There is no god but God and Muhammad is the Messenger of God', is actually to live by the moral and ethical principles of Islam. Moreover, Islam does not separate life into different compartments, each unrelated to the others, but presents an integrated and holistic world-view where everything – politics, science, social affairs, public life – is subject to its ethical and moral precepts. Thus, Islam and politics go hand in hand; and all Muslims, by the very nature of their faith, are political activists. What this means is that Muslims have consciously to work to establish a just and equitable community and be perpetually on guard against oppression and unjust rule.

Given that nationalism is anathema to Islam, and the fact that the Prophet Muhammad spent his entire life eradicating tribalism from the Arabian society of his time, how do we account for the emergence of nationalism in the Muslim world? Can the virulent strain of Muslim nationalism so evident in the Middle East and South Asia be justified in Islamic terms? Is theirs a relationship between nationalism and the rise of Islamic fundamentalism? And what does the future hold both for fundamentalism and Muslim nationalism?

One of the paradoxes of recent Muslim history is that the emergence of nationalism in the Muslim world is connected to the rise of modern Islamic reform movements. In the late nineteenth century, Jamaludding Afghani (d. 1897), together with Mohammed Abduh (d. 1905), the Grand Mufti of Egypt, founded the Salafi movement. Afghani and Abduh wanted to modernize Islam and campaigned to establish a pan-Islamic movement, cutting tribal and national lines, across the Muslim world. A series of writers, loyal to Afghani and Abduh, and inspired by their vision of a modernized Islam, put forward new ideas about the way in which society and state should be organized. They saw modernity largely in terms of Western modes of thought and social organization. It was in the generation following Afghani and Abduh, in the early part of the twentieth century, that nationalism became explicit amongst Arabs, particularly the Egyptians and Tunisians, and the Turks. In adopting the idea of nationalism *à la Europe*, it was inevitable that they should give it some local colouring. Thus 'religious nationalism', 'regional nationalism', 'cultural nationalism' and 'ethnic nationalism' were all proclaimed.[1] Initially, there was no clear-cut division between these brands, and Islam was always there in implicit if not in explicit forms. But by the beginning of the 1920s a more linguistic and racially based nationalism came to the fore.

The various national movements arose in response to different challenges. In Egypt, nationalism emerged as a reaction to both European colonialism and traditional Islam, which was seen as backward and obscurantist, as well as to the rediscovery of pre-Islamic Egyptian history. When, in 1922, the tomb of Tutankhaman was discovered and opened, it generated considerable interest in Pharaonic history and the pre-Islamic identity of Egypt. Ahmad Shawqi, who was a court poet during the era of Muhammad Ali, became the spokesperson of Egyptian nationalism which drew inspiration from the Pharaonic past of Egypt. Thus Egyptian nationalism emerged as an attempt to end British occupation, and had a specific Egyptian (Pharaonic) rather an Islamic or Arab content. In Lebanon, nationalism was introduced by Arab Christians who sought a greater measure of autonomy under the protection of European powers.[2] In Syria and Palestine, Muslims and Christians live together, and the emphasis was put on their common 'national bond'. Turkish nationalism grew out of the continuing decline and eventual collapse of the Caliphate and Ottoman empire, as well as the persistent and growing pressure from Europe. Kemal Ataturk and the Young Turks were aggressively anti-Islamic, and saw Islam as a hindrance to the modernization of Turkey. Turkish nationalism was based on pride in being a Turk and on total and complete imitation of Europe. In contrast, Muslim nationalism in the Indian sub-continent had strong Islamic roots. Indian Muslim leaders, like the poet and philosopher Muhammad Iqbal, felt that the Islamic identity of Muslims of India would be submerged in an India dominated by Hindus. The whole *raison d'être* of the Pakistan movement was to have a separate homeland for Muslims where their identity and religion could be protected. However, one thing all national movements agreed upon, and all varieties of nationalism shared: the idea that European political theory, with the nation state as its base, was the model to follow.

Initially, the Islamic movements took an anti-nationalism stand. The Jamaat-e-Islami, for example, was originally against Muslim nationalism and the idea of Pakistan, but after the creation of Pakistan, nationalism became an unconscious part of its agenda. The idea of Islam and state also became intrinsically linked. Pakistan was created as the 'first Islamic state'; it followed that Islam was both the religion of the state and the state. The 'Islamic state' was to be ruled by the *Shariah*, or Islamic law, and the best rulers of the 'Islamic state' could only be those who had knowledge and expertise in Islamic law and who were recognized by the populace as the true guardians of Islam: the *ulama* or the religious scholars. During the 1950s, 1960s and 1970s, Islamic movements throughout the Muslim world were engaged in an intense struggle for the establishment of 'Islamic states', dominated, if not totally ruled, by the *ulamas*. On the whole, this endeavour was based on democratic means with emphasis on organization of cells of devoted and loyal activists. But the arrival of fundamentalism changed all that.

Fundamentalism is a direct result of the failure of secular nationalism in the Muslim world and the imported European modernity on which it was based. Dictatorial nation states stripped Muslim societies of their plurality by marginalizing all except the Westernized elites from power and ruthlessly suppressing all minorities. Modernity stripped Muslim communities of their protective, insulating layer of tradition and civic society. Neither nationalism nor modernity recognized or addressed the basic sources of the suffering of Muslim people. Ill-fitting modernization and development schemes destroyed the very foundation of traditional lifestyles. Displaced from their land and unable to sustain themselves, millions of farmers and rural folk were, and still are, forced to migrate to overcrowded cities, without infrastructure, adequate housing, sanitation or employment.[3] Depravation and bitterness breeds extremism; when it is combined with a strong sense of religious identity, fundamentalism is the lethal product.

Where nationalism and modernity have failed spectacularly, fundamentalism has inspired many Muslims with its successes. The Iranian revolution demonstrated to Islamists everywhere that armed struggle pays when the Islamic movement is faced by an oppressive secular state. The success of *mujahideen* in Afghanistan showed that pure religious will can overpower a superpower. The religiously based *intifada* in Palestine, as well as the Muslim militants in Lebanon, in sharp contrast to nationalists, provide evidence that tables can be turned on those who refuse to listen to just Muslim demands. And where secularists would not allow democratic representation of Islam, as in Algeria, Islam can be brought in through the back door – with the help of the military, as in the Sudan and the Pakistan of General Zia.

However, despite its apparent successes, fundamentalism has turned out to be just as oppressive and authoritarian as naked secular nationalism: Iran and the Sudan provide a good demonstration of the oppressive capability of fundamentalism. This *has* to be so, as fundamentalism is the product of exactly the same dynamic as secular nationalism. Islamic fundamentalism is not based on a classical religious narrative or Muslim tradition: it has no historical precedence. It is a modern, concocted dogma. It uses both religious chauvinism and nationalism for the formulation of an ahistoric social identity. It combines the retrieval of the constructed romantic and puritan past with the modernist ideal of a nation confined in a territorial nation state to generate a wholly new religious and political outlook.

Islam is pre-eminently a doctrine of truth. In the fundamentalist purview, believing in the truth of Islam is equated with *possessing* the truth. Thus fundamentalists, claiming that only their version of Islam is the absolute truth, not only deny the manifest diversity and plurality of Islam, but also arrogate divine powers to themselves. What distinguishes fundamentalism from traditional Islam, as Parvez Manzoor has argued so convincingly, is that 'the cognitive theory of "state" is "fundamental" to its vision of Islam and represents a paramount fact of its consciousness'. Thus, from a 'totalistic theocentric world-view, a God-centred way of life and thought, of knowledge and action', Islam is transformed into a 'totalitarian theocratic world order that submits every human situation to the arbitration of the state'.[4] When society and state become one, politics disappears, cultural and social spaces are totally homogenized, and the end-product mirrors Fascism. When Islam is transformed into an exclusivist ideology, the sacred is politicized and politics becomes sacred, everything is bulldozed into a quasi-Fascist uniformity. The fundamentalist interpretation of Islam not only does violence to its tradition, history and pluralistic outlook, but has no solution to offer the modern world. Fundamentalism is, in the words of Manzoor, 'all cause and no programme', and thus superfluous and irrelevant to contemporary times.

This fabricated dogma of Islam-as-fundamentalism is very much a minority phenomenon in the Muslim world. Most fundamentalist organizations, as their very names suggest, encircle a minority to the exclusion of the majority: 'The Muslim Brotherhood', 'Hizbullah' ('The Party of God'), Gamaa-el-Islam (the Egyptian 'The Party of Islam'). The very nature of these insular movements, based as they are on the retrieval of an imagined 'pristine' beginnings, leads them to engage with the world in terms of dichotomies: fundamentalism versus modernism, normativism versus acculturationism, revivalism versus re-entrenchment, Islam versus the West. Thus everything must be rejected; and the rejection begins by cutting off ties with the West and all its ills and ends with intolerance of all interpretations of Islam which differ from those of the clan. Similar ideas lead to a total rejection of democracy. But democracy, or indeed any notion, Western or non-Western, clashes with Islam only when it conceives itself as a doctrine of truth or violates one of the fundamental notions of Islam. Only when democracy becoms wedded to atheistic humanism and lays claims to being a dogma of truth, or when secularism interprets itself as an epistemology, does it clash with the faith of Islam. As a mechanism for representative government, devoid of its ideological pretensions and trappings, democracy has no quarrel with Islam. But fundamentalism is too one-dimensional to make such distinctions.

It is because of its exclusivist and one-dimensional outlook, as well as its intrinsic connection with an idealized nation state of Islam, that fundamentalism has no long-term future. An Islamic party or government that comes to power by force and rules by terror, violence and intrigue is a contradiction in terms. It is anti-Islamic, and its anti-Islamic nature will eventually become evident to all Muslims. Witness how all those who initially welcomed and supported the Iranian revolution now reject the theocratic and totalitarian states it has created. It is also worth pointing out that in Islam there is no difference between ends and means: an Islamic goal can only be achieved by Islamic means. Thus only through *ijma* (consensus) and *shura* (consultation), the two fundamental concepts of Islamic political theory, can a true Islamic polity be established. The global decline of the sovereignty of the nation state will also make fundamentalism superfluous. 'Our world is beginning to resemble,' as John Keane notes,

> the *form* of the mediaeval world, in which monarchs were forced to share power and authority with a variety of subordinate and higher powers. The trend has profound implications for the struggle for an Islamic state. It renders implausible the revolutionary strategy of seizing state power, if need be through the use of force, precisely because the centres of state power are tending to become more dispersed and, hence, immune from 'capture' by a single party or government. Not only that, but insofar as 'the state' ceases to be in one place to be 'seized' the struggle by Islamists to monopolize state is rendered unnecessary.[5]

Nationalism itself, however, will continue to play an important part in the Muslim world for the next few decades, not least because the end of the Cold War has unleashed nationalist sentiments in the Muslim communities of Central Asia. The war was cold because it froze history in Europe and abandoned the fate of some 150 million Muslims to Communism. The emergence of the six new Islamic republics in central Asia – Azerbaijan, Kazakhstan, Kyrgyztan, Tadjikistan, Turkmenistan and Uzbekistan – as well as Albania and Bosnia-Herzegovina, has provided impetus for Muslims in Russia and China to follow suit. Despite all the efforts, it would not be possible to curb the tide of nationalism and the desire of Muslim regions in Russia for old-fashioned liberation. The war in Chechenia is an indication of what is to follow: there will be nationalist struggles for independence in Dagestan, Abkhazia, Adzhar, Kabardino-Balkar and Tatraristan within the next decade. Nationalist movements will also emerge in southern China, particularly in the province of Xinjiang.

However, contrary to conventional belief, the emergence of Muslim nationalism in Central Asia will hasten the demise of mindless fundamentalism. It will also increase the pressure on older Muslim states to produce real Islamic alternatives to oppressive forms of modernity and come up with more participatory forms of governance. The more established parties of the Islamic movement, like the Muslim Brotherhood and Jamaat-e-Islami of Pakistan, have already foreseen this future. These organizations have now started to concentrate their efforts on social and intellectual reform and developing alternative models and policies for solving the pressing problems of poverty, unemployment and social dislocation. Traditional communities are being empowered in areas of life underneath and outside the state, thus laying the foundation for a future transition to more consensus-orientated, consultative and democratic forms of Islamic polity.[6]

Imported and imposed European nationalism and modernity disenfranchised a large segment of the global Muslim community – the *ummah* – and took it to extremes of poverty and social and cultural dislocation. Fundamentalism emerged as a gut reaction against modernity and pushed more militant elements in Muslim communities to the other extreme. The Muslims now know from experience that neither offers positive solutions to their problems. The emerging, new discourse in Muslim societies is about 'the middle path' as emphasized by the Qur'an: 'And thus we have willed you to be a community of the middle way, so that with your lives you might bear witness with truth before humanity' (2.143).

Notes

1. A. L. Tibawi, *Arabic and Islamic Themes*, London 1976, ch. 5, 'From Islam to Arab Nationalism', 99–153.

2. A. Hourani, *A History of the Arab Peoples*, London 1991, 308–11.

3. For a fascinating account of how this process has worked see D. Hillel, *Rivers of Eden*, London 1994.

4. S. Parvez Manzoor, 'The Future of Muslim Politics: Critique of the "Fundamentalist" Theory of the Islamic State', *Futures* 23.3, 1991, 289–301.

5. John Keane, 'Power Sharing Islam?', in Azzam Tamimi (ed.), *Power Sharing Islam*, London 1993, 22.

6. For a detailed exploration of this new discourse see Ziauddin Sardar, *Islamic Futures: The Shape of Ideas to Come*, London 1985; and the special issue on 'Islam and the Future' of *Futures* 23.3, 1991.

Contributors

HEINZ SCHILLING was born in 1942 in Bergneustadt, Rhineland. After studying history, German, philosophy and sociology in Cologne and Freiburg, he gained his doctorate in 1971 with *Niederländische Exulanten im 16. Jahrhundert. Ihre Stellung im Sozialgefüge und im religiösen Leben deutscher und englischer Städte*, Gütersloh 1972. From 1971 to 1977 he was academic assistant in the faculty of history at the University of Bielefeld, where he gained his Habilitation with *Konfessionskonflikt und Staatsbildung in frühneuzeitlichen Deutschland*, Gütersloh 1981. From 1977 to 1982 he was professor of early modern history at the University of Giessen, from 1982 to 1992 professor at the University of Giessen, and since 1992 he has been professor at the Humboldt University in Berlin. Address: Institut für Geschichten-Wissenschaften, Unter den Linden 6, 10099 Berlin, Germany.

VICTOR CONZEMIUS was born in 1929 in Echternach, Luxembourg and studied history, philosophy and theology in Fribourg, Switzerland and in Paris. After gaining his doctorate in Fribourg, in 1955 he was ordained priest. Between 1965 and 1968 he lectured in modern history at University College, Dublin, and in 1970 he became Professor of Church History at Lucerne. He retired in 1980 and since then has worked free-lance. Books include *Katholizismus ohne Rom. Die alt-katholische Kirchengemeinschaft*, Zurich 1969; *Eglises chrétiennes et totalitarisme nationalsocialiste*, Louvain 1969; *Propheten und Vorläufer. Wegbereiter des neuzeitlichen Katholizismus*, Zurich 1972; *Philipp Anton von Segesser. Demokrat zwischen den Fronten*, Zurich 1977. He has also edited the correspondence of Ignaz Döllinger (4 vols.), Munich 1963–81, and the letters of P. A. von Segesser (6 vols.), Zurich 1983–95. Address: Schädrütihalde 12, CH 6006 Luzern, Switzerland.

MIKLÓS TOMKA was born in 1941; he studied economics and sociology in Budapest, Leuven and Leiden, and taught in Budapest, where he is now Professor of the Sociology of Religion. He has also been a visiting professor

in Bamberg and Innsbruck. A co-founder of the Hungarian Pastoral Institute (in 1989), he is also Director of the Hungarian Catholic Social Academy and head of the Hungarian Religious Research Centre (both also from the same year).
Address: H–1171 Budapest, Váviz u.4, Hungary.

HEINRICH SCHNEIDER was born in 1929 in Brandenburg, Germany. He studied in Bamberg, Cleveland, Ohio and Munich, where he gained his doctorate in 1955. He has been active in the European Movement and the Tutzing Academy for Political Education (of which he was Deputy Director), and was professor of Political Sciences in Hanover (until 1968). He was then Professor of Political Philosophy in the University of Vienna from 1968 to 1971 and Professor of Political Science in the University of Bonn from 1971 to 1991. He has written over 200 works on European politics, security and political theory, and is editor of the quarterly *Integration*.
Address: Doktorberg 3/4, A2391 Kaltenleutgeben, Austria.

JOHN A. COLEMAN SJ was born in San Francisco in 1937. He holds advanced degrees in sociology from the University of California, Berkeley, and did advanced study in theology at the University of Chicago. He is the author or editor of over ten books, including *An American Strategic Theology*. He serves as the editor-in-chief for the Isaac Haecker series in American culture and religion and is currently Professor of Religion and Society at the Graduate Theological Union in Berkeley, California.
Address: The Jesuit School of Theology at Berkeley, 1735 LeRoy Avenue, Berkeley, CA 94709, USA.

SRDJAN VRCAN is emeritus Professor of Sociology in the University of Split, Croatia. He was formerly Co-Director of the Seminar on the Future of Religion at the Inter-University Centre for Graduate Studies, Dubrovnik. He has written *Od Krize religije do religije krize* (From the Crisis of Religion to the Religion of Crisis) and is co-author of *Raspeto katolicanstvo* (Catholicism at the Crossroads), both published in Zagreb, along with many articles on religion.
Address: Bartola Kasica 30, 58000 Split, Croatia.

DAVID SELJAK was born in 1958 in Toronto, Ontario, Canada. He is currently a lecturer in religion and the social sciences at the Faculty of Religious Studies at McGill University in Montreal, Quebec. His PhD

dissertation concerns the reaction of the Catholic Church in Quebec to the
new secular nationalism of the 1960s and 1970s. He has published a
number of articles on religion and nationalism.
Address: McGill University, Faculty of Religious Studies, 3520 University Street, Montreal PQ H3A 2A7, Canada.

GREGORY BAUM was born in Berlin in 1923; since 1940 he has lived in
Canada. He studied at McMaster University, Hamilton; Ohio State
University; the University of Fribourg and the New School for Social
Research, New York. He is now Professor of Theology and Social Ethics at
McGill University, Montreal. He is editor of *The Ecumenist*; his books
include *Religion and Alienation* (1975), *The Social Imperative* (1978),
Catholics and Canadian Socialism (1980), *The Priority of Labor* (1982),
Ethics and Economics (1984) and *Theology and Society* (1987).
Address: McGill University, 3520 University St, Montreal H3A 2A7.

ASHIS NANDY, who was born in 1937, is Fellow and Director of the Centre
for the Study of Developing Societies and Chairman of the Committee for
Cultural Choices and Global Futures. He is a political psychologist and
sociologist of science. His books include *At the Edge of Psychology* (1980),
The Initimate Enemy. Loss and Recovery of Self Under Colonialism
(1983), *Traditions, Tyranny and Utopias* (1987), *The Tao of Cricket*
(1987) and *The Illegitimacy of Nationalism* (1994). He has also edited
Science, Hegemony and Violence and is co-author of *The Blinded Eye: 500
Years of Christopher Columbus* (1993). He has been a visiting fellow in
Washington DC, Hull and Edinburgh, a visiting professor at the
University of Texas in Austin, and has held the first UNESCO Chair at
the Centre for European Studies in Trier.
Address: N. Flat 16, 32 Alipur Road, Delhi 110054, India.

ZIAUDDIN SARDAR, writer, broadcaster and cultural critic, is Professor of
Science and Technology Policy, Middlesex University. He is the author of
24 books including *The Future of Muslim Civilization, Islamic Futures:
The Shape of Ideas of Come, Information and the Muslim World,
Explorations in Islamic Science*; as co-author, *Distorted Imagination:
Lessons from the Rushdie Affair, Barbaric Others: A Manifesto on Western
Racism* and *Muhammad for Beginners*; and as editor *The Touch of Midas:
Science, Values and the Environment in Islam and the West, The Revenge
of Athena: Science, Exploitation and the Third World* and *Muslim
Minorities in Western Societies*. A consulting editor of *Futures*, the

monthly journal of forecasting, planning and policy, he is a regular contributor to the literary pages of *The Independent*. His most recent television programme was 'Islamic Conversation' which was broadcast on Britain's Channel 4 during 1994.

Address: 1 Orchard Gate, London NW9, UK.

Members of the Advisory Committee for Sociology of Religion

Concilium Subscription Information - outside North America

Individual Annual Subscription (six issues): £30.00

Institution Annual Subscription (six issues): £40.00

Airmail subscriptions: add £10.00

Individual issues: £8.95 each

New subscribers please return this form:
for a two-year subscription, double the appropriate rate

(for individuals)   £30.00   (1/2 years)   . . . .

(for institutions)   £40.00   (1/2 years)   . . . .

Airmail postage
outside Europe +£10.00   (1/2 years)   . . . .

Total . . . .

I wish to subscribe for one/two years as an individual/institution
(delete as appropriate)

Name/Institution . . . .

Address . . . .

. . . .

. . . .

I enclose a cheque for . . . . payable to SCM Press Ltd

Please charge my Access/Visa/Mastercard no. . . . .

Signature . . . . .Expiry Date . . . .

Please return this form to:
SCM PRESS LTD 26-30 Tottenham Road, London N1 4BZ